A TALE OF
TWO BIRDS

OTHER BOOKS BY GORDON B. GREER

World in Conflict
The First Decade
What Price Security
All-Weather Fighters
The Role of Luck

A TALE OF
TWO BIRDS

GORDON B. GREER

iUniverse, Inc.
New York   Bloomington

A TALE OF TWO BIRDS

iUniverse books may be ordered through booksellers or by contacting:

iUniverse
1663 Liberty Drive
Bloomington, IN 47403
www.iuniverse.com
1-800-Authors (1-800-288-4677)

Because of the dynamic nature of the Internet, any Web addresses or links contained
in this book may have changed since publication and may no longer be valid. The
views expressed in this work are solely those of the author and do not necessarily
reflect the views of the publisher, and the publisher hereby disclaims any responsibility
for them.

ISBN: 978-1-4401-1020-7 (sc)
ISBN: 978-1-4401-1021-4 (ebook)
ISBN: 978-1-4401-1022-1 (dj)

Printed in the United States of America

iUniverse rev. date: 12/18/2008

CONTENTS

ACKNOWLEDGEMENTS

The staff of the Information Technologies Department of Bingham McCutchen, and particularly Dennis Scheffler, has done its usual job of keeping my word processing equipment processing words. Our son, Bruce, an excellent military historian, has made a number of very helpful suggestions for this book. My wife, Nancy, has been very patient and helpful throughout the writing process. The staff of the publisher has done its usual good job of converting my efforts into an attractive format.

Any errors in the following material are mine alone.

Belmont, Massachusetts
2008

A Tale Of Two Birds

One may be the best of birds, the other some think may be the worst of birds. They are both named Osprey one of which is feathered and the other is fabricated although, apart from both being able to fly and having had life-threatening problems, their names are their only similarity. Their stories will be told anon but first a great deal of context is necessary.

Background

The written history of Western warfare with any claim to accuracy probably dates from 1299 B.C.E.[1] with the Egyptian account of the battle of Kedesh in what is now Syria. The battle was between the Egyptian New Kingdom to the south and the New Hittite Kingdom located in Anatolia.[2] The only extant version of the battle is from an Egyptian description carved in stone. It describes the battle as an Egyptian triumph although by a narrow margin. Given the events which occurred following the battle there is some thought that the battle may have been a draw or even an Egyptian loss.[3] The Egyptians appeared never to have moved north of the battlefield and the subsequently created dividing line between the two great powers was slightly south of the battlefield. For our purposes it is not important to determine who won and who lost or whether the only description was probably propaganda of a particularly remarkable duration. It is only important that the battle was described. We have therefore some glimmerings, however cryptic and biased, of the tactics employed.

Most subsequent historians described battles more fully and seemingly more accurately, sometimes as contemporaneous events, sometimes even battles in which the historians were participants. Of course the participation by the historians did not mean they were unbiased in their accounts. Perhaps those historians were more biased by virtue either of their participation or of their knowledge of subsequent events. Nevertheless we do have accounts of battles from Homer (his blindness and his works having been composed at least 400 years after the events of course precluded the subjects of

---

1   Before the Common Era, the now more politically correct version of B.C. (Before Christ)

2   The author is aware of the irony of beginning a discussion of largely Western warfare with a battle between an Asian country (located roughly in modern-day Asiatic Turkey) and an African country.

3   Kinder and Hilgemann, *The Atlas of World History*, vol. I (1974), p. 35.

any of his works being of the eye-witnessed variety). Those accounts, being poetic and colorful, seem to be at least as much art as fact. A somewhat similar deviation from literal fact in military history (via a nationalistic and/or a morality bias) seemed to be at least a major component of Herodotus of Halicarnassus' *History of the Persian Wars*. Notwithstanding Cicero's sobriquet for Herodotus as the Father of History, Thucydides' *History of the Peloponnesian War* was probably the beginning of more or less objective reporting of military history.[4] Bias and misinformation still abounded, but going forward in time from those fifth century B.C.E. writers we tend to have a better chance of identifying weapons and tactics, although causes and results of battles and wars may still be obscure. Following Thucydides there were an increasing number of reports of battles, among them were reports on the campaigns of Alexander the Great, the detailed but exaggerated and self-serving accounts by Julius Caesar of his many triumphs in the Gallic and Civil Wars and various accounts of 400 years of border wars between the Western Roman Empire and barbarian tribes, in the aggregate covering the next eight centuries or so after the Peloponnesian War.

It is probably obvious that neither changes in tactics nor in weapons necessarily occur rapidly. It also seems reasonable that major changes in early weapons took a long time to be put into use. Consider a major change in weapons that occurred around the beginning of the period being discussed. The first metal weapons used by armies in the Middle East were made of bronze metal, which is a mixture of copper and tin. Those metals were fairly easily worked and copper was widely distributed. Tin, on the other hand, was quite rare in the Middle East. Somehow the ancient Britons discovered large tin deposits which were converted into primitive mines, some of which were still being worked as late as the twentieth century. They would have known that tin was very useful in making the most important metal of the era, known to historians as the Bronze Age. The information about the

---

4   Thucydides was described as the "wisest of historians and much readable" by Rear Admiral Eller, USN, in his Introduction to Morison, *History of United States Naval Operations in World War II*, vol. XV (1961), p. vii.

existence and location of English tin mines soon filtered back to the Middle East. A considerable trade grew up in English tin, carried by ships sailing in part through North Atlantic waters. Those seas were much more dangerous than was the usual case in the Mediterranean Sea but somehow the sailors managed to make the voyage. It was remarkable that so much was known in the ancient world about the very remote British Isles almost 2,000 years before Julius Caesar led the first Roman invasion there. This tin trade brought the British into at least some part of the ambit of Western civilization long before the period that their presence there was usually assumed. This rather undermines the idea that the outlying parts of Europe were very primitive and were waiting for the Romans or some other benefactors to arrive and pull them out of barbarism. At any rate, copper from the Middle East and tin from England did unite on a regular basis by about halfway through the reigns of the Egyptian pharaohs, although Egypt obviously had found a limited amount of tin earlier because some bronze items dating from at least a thousand years earlier have been found in Egyptian ruins.

Bronze weapons remained the rule in Egypt until the Egyptians came in close contact with the Hittites. The Hittites home territory in the area then known as Anatolia was rich in iron ore and in some cases actual iron. The Hittites had learned how to purify the iron and to work the resulting metal. Consistent with the times, they soon began to make iron weapons. This, of course, did not all happen quickly for metallurgy was far more luck than science at the time. Eventually the Hittites armed themselves with iron weapons which were the cutting edge (sorry) of armament at the time and were far superior to the bronze swords, spear points and arrowheads of their enemy, Egypt. Egypt, of course, tried to make iron but it took time to find iron ore and to learn how to derive iron from it. It also took the Hittites some time to equip their whole army suitably with iron weapons. Although tactics in war can be changed almost overnight and can generally be taught to the troops quickly, it may have taken generations after its discovery of iron for each country to produce sufficient weapons to arm their troops suitably. Whatever the time table, the Hittites were ahead. Unfortunately their lead in iron weapons did not permit them to dominate Anatolia for much longer. In less than a hundred years after the battle at Kedesh the Hittite Empire was gone.

The point of listing some of the early historical sources of battle descriptions for the 800 years of Greek and Roman activity is not to debate the results of those battles or the accuracy of the accounts but rather to recognize from those accounts that tactics and weapons did not vary much over the almost two millennia between the battle at Kedesh and the collapse of the Western Roman Empire.

Most major battles in this 800 year period were fought principally with infantry. The soldiers were armed with swords, mainly short, and/or spears and pikes; the auxiliary troops were often armed with bows and arrows or slings. The soldiers usually wore a metal or leather helmet and had body armor of one sort or another; the auxiliary troops were usually unarmored. The weapons were made of wood, iron and, rarely, steel and the formations were very close order. The reason their swords were usually short was because most battles were fought with the contestants in those very close formations. There was not much room in such formations to swing a long sword in order to inflict slashing wounds on one's enemy so thrusting strokes ahead at one's enemy was a usual battle tactic, as was simply trying to push your enemy backwards. For this type of stroke a short, sharp-pointed sword was best. Spears and pikes were also used and were most effective weapons when placed in a stationary position with the enemy moving toward them. Of course if both sides in a battle adopted this tactic not much would happen. There was a convention until a few hundred years ago that the results of battles were not determined so much by inflicting more casualties on one's enemy than one received but rather by which force occupied the battlefield at the end of the day. The fighting to capture the battlefield was then done by jabbing, not swinging, weapons to force one's enemy backward, at least during the early stages of a battle. Since spears and pikes were most useful in a fixed or very slowly moving formation in which the weapons were arranged so as to prevent an enemy from getting past the points of the weapons, spear-carrying soldiers would have little defense against an enemy that managed to avoid the tips of the spears. In fact, in later battles involving troops with pikes (simply longer and heavier spears) a tactic often used was for the infantry which was opposed by pikemen to get under the pike points and push the pikes upwards and out of the way. In trying to push a 15 to 18 foot pike upward, a foot soldier had enormous leverage over the pikeman who would be trying to keep the pike level by holding the pike shaft at the end. If the lifting tactic worked the pikeman would be left with two hands on the pike trying to bring it back down to level where it would be effective while he was being attacked by the sword-carrying enemy infantry. If several pikemen were to drop their pikes to try to defend themselves with sword or knife they would create a gap in the pike formation which might result in serious, perhaps fatal, consequences to the formation.

Quite obviously battle formations and tactics did not remain entirely static for the period. What would seem to us as quite minor changes were made to the weapons and the tactics during this period especially when compared to the changes of the last 100 years. Nonetheless the basic concepts of battle and of armament and armor remained rather stable. Although changes in battle techniques did occur in this period their paucity and relative unimportance indicate a general stability. While battle line against battle line suggests a simplicity of training, a macho philosophy (we are stronger or more mobile or both than they are) and an ease of control, there were exceptions. We know that at least as far back as Alexander the Great tactical envelopment movements were executed. These involved using a part of one's forces to hit the enemy on its flank or, if possible, in its rear where the enemy would be particularly vulnerable. In the process the attacker would try to insure that his enemy did not know of his plans lest the enemy attack the area which had been weakened by the diversion of the forces assigned to do the envelopment. Many envelopments were made by cavalry because of its ability to move rapidly as well as the sometimes less effectiveness of direct cavalry attacks against strong infantry formations. Alexander the Great's use of envelopments was particularly impressive because he was usually fighting against large odds and was thus taking great risks by diverting some of his relatively small forces to accomplish those tactics. A century after Alexander in the second Punic War, the Romans were fighting an invading Carthaginian army commanded by Hannibal for control of central Italy. At the battle of Cannae (in 216 B.C.E.) the Carthaginians slipped around both sides of the large Roman force (a double envelopment) and destroyed the Roman army. The double envelopment movement may well have been used before but probably not in as important a situation and with such dramatic consequences.

A whole separate category of warfare has been a significant part of military history for millennia. That is siege warfare. When castles, forts and walled cities were involved the weapons and tactics of field armies were of very limited use. Captures of strong fortifications have been reported in some detail at least as far back as the siege of Troy in the Iliad and as modern as the capture of the Belgian border forts by the Germans at the beginning of World War II. The techniques for the construction and operation of such fortifications show a great deal of practical engineering knowledge as did the engines and techniques used by besiegers. While often effective sieges have been an ugly litany of human cruelty over thousands of years. From poisoning and stopping water supplies of the besieged, both military and civilian, to throwing huge stones into and over the walls, to throwing diseased animals and humans over the walls to spread disease inside, the besiegers waged indiscriminate war on all living beings within their target.[5] Eventually gunpowder got into the act to blow openings in the fortifications. Since this aspect of warfare does not touch upon the principal points of this book it will not be covered in any detail here. It should be noted, however, that many of the particularly ingenious devices developed in the two millennia beginning with Archimedes and ending with Leonardo da Vinci were related to sieges. Both the besiegers and the besieged were greatly helped by specially constructed machines but those

---

5   It is not generally realized that the besiegers had their own problems with disease which often caused sieges to be lifted and the besieging army to be dispersed. When the attacking troops finally broke into a city it is not surprising that they were usually quite violent in their treatment of the inhabitants, both military and civilian.

machines were both heavy and complicated, at least by the standards of the time. This tended to limit their use to stationary situations like sieges. Additionally the descriptions of the form and use of some of these devices are also of dubious veracity. Accordingly, while mention is made of them here since they are not part of the mainline of the history of weapons they will not be discussed further.

It is a truism of military history that wars are often begun with at least one side and often both sides using the tactics of the prior war. The previous winner will probably continue with its tactics that had worked successfully before; the loser may have adopted the winner's tactics or tried to develop its own tactics to counter the previous winner's tactics. The more recent history of warfare, particularly that of the six centuries preceding the twentieth century, began slowly to be made up to a some degree by the thrust and parry of new or improved weapons and new tactics. What seemed to have been happening was that often after a war was over the military thinkers of the world would spend the following period of peace studying the winning tactics and, if applicable, the winning weapons used in that war. In the early part of those 600 years, with one very major exception, there tended to be little development in weapons so changes in warfare were more likely to result from changes in tactics than from improvements in weapons. This was the case in both land and sea warfare but in most cases those tactical changes seem to have been quite minimal. In the spirit of static tactics, during part of this period the Royal Navy even went so far as to specify in standing orders what actions its admirals and captains should take or not take in a range of circumstances in battle. An officer who violated these rules was at risk of serious punishment. It was bad enough in some situations that these rules provided a tactical straightjacket for the officers of the Royal Navy but, because most potential enemies would also know what the rules provided, they would know a good deal about how the English fleet would act in a number of battle conditions. This was obviously a significant advantage to Britain's adversaries. Fortunately for the Royal Navy it could usually concede to its opponents some such advantages and still prevail. Also fortunately for the Royal Navy not every British naval commander followed these Admiralty instructions. The leading heretic in this respect during the late eighteenth and very early nineteenth centuries was Horatio Nelson, both when he was a ship's captain and more dramatically when he was an admiral commanding a fleet or a portion of a fleet. He also, on occasion, was known for his ignoring of direct orders from his superiors. It would have been extremely awkward for his commanding officers to punish him for not following the rules or orders when he won his battles.[6] Although Nelson regularly got away with violating the Admiralty's rules without punishment, he was not rewarded as well as he thought he deserved to be for his victories. If indeed he had not been adequately rewarded it was more likely to have happened as a result of the conduct of his personal life, which offended some more senior officers, than of his conduct in battle and in ignoring orders.

The Royal Navy was not consistent about the specificity of its orders. For many years the captains of some of His Britannic Majesty's ships were given wide latitude in the execution of their orders because of the long time they would be out of touch with the Admiralty given the distances they would be going and the situations they would find. Circumstances could, and probably would, have changed in the time between the issuance of the orders and their execution. When, toward the end of the nineteenth century, overseas telegraph messages became possible, such messages could be left for ship captains at convenient ports and, by the early years of the twentieth century, radio messages could be sent directly from the Admiralty to ships at sea. This gave initially the Admiralty an opportunity to issue much more detailed orders because it felt it could revise them as

---

6   This was, in some ways, not as bad as it might seem today. There was likely to be a delay, sometimes many months, between a commanding officer issuing an order and the subordinate receiving it at a time when the situation had changed. Sometimes a subordinate could disregard a current order because he had a better view of the situation. Nelson on at least one occasion put a telescope to his blind eye and claimed not to have seen an important signal that he felt was wrong. Nelson's judgment, at least in this instance, was correct. There was a feeling on the part of some senior officers that "any damn fool could follow orders; it took a good officer to know when to disobey them."

necessary based on information radioed to the Admiralty or to senior officers. This switch in the amount of flexibility given to officers at sea could not be better illustrated than by the standing orders in effect at the time of the Battle of Jutland which ran to 200 pages as compared to Admiral Jellicoe's predecessor's standing orders of two pages.[7] The pendulum swung back toward simple orders quite a bit in World War II at least for the most important naval battle of that war, the Battle of Midway, when "Admiral Nimitz's orders to his two commanders of carrier task forces, Fletcher and Spruance, were to 'inflict maximum damage on enemy by employing strong attrition tactics,' which in the naval language of that day meant air strikes on enemy ships. He cannily ordered Fletcher and Spruance to take initial positions to the northeastward of Midway, beyond search range of the approaching enemy, anticipating that the 700-mile searches by Midway-based planes would locate the Japanese carriers before the presence of his own would be divulged. To this he added a special Letter of Instruction:-'In carrying out the task assigned . . . you will be governed by the principle of calculated risk, which you shall interpret to mean the avoidance of exposure of your force to attack by superior enemy forces without good prospect of inflicting, as a result of such exposure, greater damage on the enemy."[8]

On land as well as at sea there were few major changes in tactics until the nineteenth century. This was a little surprising. While there had not been many changes in weapons used on land, a few of those changes that had occurred had been important. Those changes had been the introduction and improvement of various firearms into war, beginning even before the 600-year period had begun with great improvements of the weapons thereafter. Before exploring firearms some mention should, however, be made of a more mundane and seldom discussed development – the stirrup.

---

7   Hough, *Great Naval Battles of the 20th Century* (2001), p. 112.

8   Morison, *History of United States Naval Operations in World War II*, vol. IV (1967), p. 84.

For our purposes here we shall count as stirrups only those devices made of metal, wood or leather which were attached to a saddle and were used to contain the feet of the rider on a continuous basis. There had been something like a single stirrup used as an aid to mounting and dismounting for centuries before true stirrups had appeared in Europe. The dual stirrups, which seemed to have appeared first in Europe at about 650 C.E,[9] made a very significant difference in mounted warfare. Stirrups of course made the rider's seat in the saddle much more secure, particularly in battle when the rider would be engaged in violent activities. They also greatly assisted the rider in two particularly military activities. The first of these activities, using a lance, perhaps surprisingly had not historically necessarily required stirrups. A system of bracing the end of the lance into the wooden part of the saddle served for some time as an assistance to the bearer of the lance but when stirrups became common the rider could use his lance with much more flexibility. While some sources feel that this was the most important result of the use of stirrups, that may be incorrect. The most important military advantage of stirrups may well have been to permit the rider to remain firmly on his horse while using a long sword to attack the enemy's troops on the ground. Although the Roman type of short sword might have been of use to a mounted man fighting another mounted man similarly armed, it was difficult to use it against men on foot, particularly if they went to ground as the cavalry rode by. The solution was obviously to equip the horsemen with longer weapons which would allow them to reach troops on the ground. The difficulty with this solution was that the horsemen would have to lean well over the side of their horses to reach the men on foot or lying on the ground and, with the action around them and their horses moving erratically, the chances of horsemen without stirrups being unseated in the process were quite good. While stirrups did not cure this problem, they minimized it quite a bit. This may well have been the greatest advantage of the use of stirrups in war.

---

9   Common Era, the now more politically correct version of A.D. (Anno Domini).

The revolution in warfare caused by the introduction of gunpowder had taken place over time and had begun slowly, at least in the western world. Gunpowder, which the Chinese had invented, made its way to Western Europe in the thirteenth century. Once the novelty of burning uncontained gunpowder and exploding it in frangible packages (later called firecrackers) had worn off, more sinister uses were planned. After the right mixture of potassium nitrate, charcoal and sulfur had been determined, the ability to cast large and strong metal containers had been developed and a satisfactory form of projectile had been found or made, the cannon was born. Initially these primitive machines were at least as dangerous to their operators as they were to any enemy but soon cannon became more useful in war, initially on land for siege purposes. Later when the cannons became smaller and more efficient they became an integral part of both army and navy warfare. Muzzle-loading gunpowder-using cannons firing solid iron shot served on naval ships for hundreds of years and changed naval warfare forever.

On land the gunpowder revolution went in three general directions. The first direction paralleled the direction of naval cannon except that most of the army guns were smaller than those of the navy because of the difficulty of moving heavy field pieces over rough or wet ground. There were two exceptions to the small cannon size on land. They were first the rare siege guns, a very large type of cannon used to knock down walls or other large structures from a fixed site and to attack enemy cannons sited in fixed areas such as forts or castles and second mortars firing a large shot at a very high angle. Large cannons were rare both because they were very difficult to make since the casting techniques of the time were not very good, particularly on the larger cannons, and because they used much power and heavy shot. The second direction of the employment of gunpowder simply used an explosive projectile which was delivered in action by lighting the fuse and throwing it at one's enemy. The device became known as a grenade (an old name for a type of fruit which it was thought to resemble) and survives to this day. The third direction was toward personal firearms, originally as a primitive form of musket but eventually becoming automatic pistols, rifles of all types and a variety of other small automatic weapons.

The first use of gunpowder in personal weapons was the introduction of hand-held firearms. There is some thought that very primitive forms of such firearms were present at the battle of Agincourt in 1415 although the English victory in that battle belonged to the English longbow. The older weapons, sword, shield, bows, lances and spears, did not disappear from the battlegrounds of Europe in a great rush even after gunpowder and weapons using it became quite widespread. In fact at the battle of Culloden, more than three centuries after the battle of Agincourt, many of the Scots armed themselves with only swords and small shields not really because they were unable to obtain and use effectively the firearms then available to infantry. The Scots favored a tactic that required them to run, preferably downhill, from just out of range of their enemy's muskets toward the enemy's lines. The effective range of the muskets in those days was not more than 100 yards and often less. That would give the musketeers time for only one shot before the Scots would be on top of them. At close quarters the sword was a far more useful weapon than the bayonet on the end of a now empty musket. Unfortunately for the Scots, in the months before Culloden the English had developed an effective counter to the Scottish tactic, the result of which limited considerably the Scottish "cold steel" approach in battles and blocked the efforts of the Scots to regain their independence.

The musket was a shoulder weapon and had, for most of its life, a smooth bore barrel. It was muzzle loaded and gunpowder powered with a succession of methods for igniting the powder charge to fire the weapon. The progression of types of ignition sequences was first the matchlock (forcing a lighted fuse into the powder charge), then the flintlock (pulling the trigger released the flint to strike iron or steel causing a spark to be generated from the flint and directed toward the powder charge) and finally the percussion cap (when hit by the hammer the cap exploded and ignited the powder charge). Each of these methods in turn improved the reliability and accuracy of the weapon. Musket bullets were generally large, round and short-ranged[10] but as rifles began to supplant muskets the bullets became smaller, more aerodynamically shaped and longer ranged. While muzzle-loading rifles had been known for quite a long time and had always been much more accurate and longer ranged than their contemporary muskets, rifles were felt to be too cumbersome and slow to load to be useful in battle. The distinction between muskets and muzzle-loading rifles became blurred in the middle of the nineteenth century with the introduction of rifled musket barrels firing more aerodynamically shaped bullets which expanded into the rifled grooves. By the latter part of the nineteenth century the rifle had become the infantry weapon of choice as rifles had become much easier to handle, due largely to breach loading with cartridges containing the smaller bullets, the propelling charge and the igniting device. Later rifles fired even smaller bullets through grooved and tighter barrels. The result was a much more accurate and longer ranged weapon. An additional important benefit, not initially very much appreciated, was that such a weapon could be quickly and easily reloaded and fired while the shooter was lying down or was in some sort of cover.

---

10 U. S. Grant, in discussing the poor performance of the muskets used by the United States Army in the Mexican War, said "A man might fire at you all day without your finding it out." Ayres, *A Military Miscellany* (2006), p. 157.

Innovation Accelerates

During the period from the initial military use of gunpowder until the beginning of the nineteenth century the changes in the military use of firearms had been slight considering the span of time covered. The firing mechanism for the musket-type weapons had evolved as described in the preceding paragraph and both artillery and naval cannons had become somewhat more reliable in terms of both their firing mechanisms and their structural components.[11]   Beyond that, major naval changes seemed to have been limited to an improved sail plan for mizzenmasts on three-masted vessels[12] and, more importantly, the use of a wheel and ropes to move the rudder in place of a tiller coupled to the rudder and connected to the steering position several decks above via a series of levers.

Until early in the nineteenth century artillery, both naval and field, fired by gunpowder solid projectiles usually made of cast iron. The principal exceptions were mortars. These were very short barreled, heavy, high fire angle cannons which lobbed large shells filled with gunpowder. The gunpowder was exploded by means of a timed fuse which was lit just before firing. The principal use of mortars was on land against land fortifications although the Royal Navy experimented briefly with their use at sea in vessels called bomb ketches.[13] The range

---

11   The search for reliability went on for a long time. The author, while in college, had a tour of a United States Army arsenal which at the time was trying to make sure that if their cannons burst they would simply split the barrel and not fracture it into pieces that would injure the gun crews.

12   Replacing the single lateen sail with a mizzen topsail over a spanker sail.

13   This use was the source of the "bombs bursting in air" language in *The Stars-Spangled Banner*. Bomb ketches were very unhandy vessels. The mortars were located forward, aimed forward and fixed in place on the ship, one on each side of the deck so as not to part the forestay when they were fired. The mortars could be aimed in azimuth only by turning the ship. Range was changed by adjusting the mortars' propelling charges. The time of explosion of the shell was set by cutting the fuse to a length that would explode the shell just as it reached

of mortars was very short and the proper timing of the fuse was quite difficult but when all went well the shells could be extremely destructive. In the 1820s the French developed a system for firing explosive shells at high velocity and low angles from ordinary artillery pieces, both naval and field. This development greatly increased the effectiveness of artillery. Naval guns now did much more than simply smash at enemy ships hoping to unseat the target's weapons, bring down its masts and kill or wound its crewmembers. This last objective was not as difficult as it might appear even when using solid shot. One did not have to hit members of a ship's crew with the shot; hits on wooden ships tended to produce large splinters which were very dangerous to the crew. This was the equivalent of the shrapnel thrown off by exploding artillery shells in a later era. Field artillery firing solid rounds (shot) did not produce the same secondary missiles although rock fragments thrown up by the shot hitting the ground could often produce casualties. On the other hand, troops in the field were usually formed into closely packed mass formations to enable their shoulder weapons and bayonets to be used in mass. Thus a cannon shot fired accurately into a formation of troops in the field would probably affect only one rank or one file of troops but the effect on that group was likely to be quite serious. Exploding shells on land threw fragments of the shells with great force and thus had a much wider effect on troops in the open. For naval purposes exploding shells not only had a serious effect on the crew and parts of the target ship but also the explosions tended to start fires. Until after the middle of the nineteenth century all western warships were made of wood and propelled by canvas sails controlled by miles of rope, all of which were highly inflammable. Onboard fires were very serious and quite often fatal.

In spite of the apparent vast improvement of artillery with exploding shells, solid shot remained in the inventory of artillery units for decades. Partially it was used for hammering blows on stone or metal targets but mainly it served to do damage when exploding shells

---

the deck of the target or touched the ground. Otherwise a brave defender could sometimes disable the fuse as the shell lay on the surface, rendering the shell harmless. Bomb ketches were not a successful class of ships.

did not explode in a timely fashion or even at all. Shells, being fragile by the standards of artillery ammunition of the day, were not very effective unless their explosive charges actually exploded at the correct time which by no means happened on every shot.[14] Thus the French invention, which some said was created to produce casualties in naval battles more approximating those of land battles,[15] was not used as much as one might think. More surprisingly, in spite of the reaction one might have expected, in land battles spreading the soldiers out on the ground rather than attacking in mass was not done. Adhering to old concepts in spite of new weapons continued into the Civil War. In one sense it could be said that exploding shells were unreliable for decades after their invention so old rules should still apply. It could also be said that the exploding shells had been adequately perfected but the minds of senior officers did not grasp the consequences for a surprisingly long time. In either case one could say that the period of gestation of exploding shells took almost half a century and the appropriate reaction to them took about the same period.

By the time the American Civil War began both land and naval forces had developed multiple shot personal gunpowder weapons but in some respects they were not perfected. Multiple shot revolvers were becoming available although most were "single action." A single action pistol could fire all of its cylinders (usually six) before having to be reloaded but the shooter must cock the hammer manually for each shot before pulling the trigger to fire the weapon. A few "double action" revolvers had been developed in the 1840s. These allowed the shooter to rotate the cylinder, cock and fire the weapon with one pull of the trigger but they were not widely used because the mechanism was complicated and at that time was quite unreliable. By the end of the Civil War a wide variety of light firearms had appeared. Among them were more accurate rifles, carbines (short barreled and light weight rifles) and an early but effective machine gun (the Gatling gun).

---

14 This may have been one of the reasons why *Monitor* used solid shot exclusively.

15 For example, the combined British, French and Spanish casualties at the Battle of Trafalgar were approximately 10% of those of the British, French and Germans at the Battle of Waterloo.

The middle of the nineteenth century was thus a major turning point in land warfare. Although the traditional doctrines had not much evolved, weapons had. Much more accurate muskets/rifles, multiple shot pistols and machine guns, more effective muzzle-loaded cannons with explosive shells and finally, after several false starts, breech-loading cannons. As had happened before, the evolution of weapons was not matched by an adequate response in the evolution of tactics.

By mid-century navies had been changed in another fundamental way. While steam propulsion for ships goes back to the end of the eighteenth century when several European inventors had built stream-powered vessels, the first practical steamship was known as *Clermont,*[16] built in 1807 by Robert Fulton and powered by paddle wheels. Steam powered tugboats driven by paddle wheels, whether located at the stern or on each side, rapidly became very useful in assisting larger ships in and out of their berths. Docking and undocking under sail with tidal flows and narrow channels had been a difficult and time-consuming task for millennia. But the use of steam as the principal motive power for ocean-going warships and merchant vessels took some time to develop. The steam engines had to become efficient enough to be able to run the planned distances on the amount of coal or wood the ship could carry. The much celebrated "steamship" SS *Savannah* made its famous transatlantic voyage in 1819 mostly under sail since she could not carry enough fuel[17] to make steam for much of the voyage. The use of steam power for ocean-going ships, especially warships, received a great boost when it was discovered that steam power could be used more efficiently by applying it to a screw propeller rather than to paddle wheels. While it was obvious that propellers under water were much less vulnerable to enemy gunfire than paddle wheels with at least half of their structure not only above water but also exposed on the outside of

---

16 Her real name was *North River Steamboat*; the name *Clermont* came later and was informal.

17 She was intended to use coal which would have been inadequate to drive her across the Atlantic but the unavailability of coal forced her to use wood, a less efficient fuel, requiring her to operate under sail for an even greater portion of her voyage than had been planned.

the ship, it was counterintuitive to most persons that propellers could apply power to the water as well as paddle wheels. The debate about this subject raged on for a few years. In the 1830s of course it was not possible to develop a computer simulation to resolve the debate. The Royal Navy solved the problem in an old-fashioned but very practical way. It built two ships identical in all respects except for the way their steam power was applied for propulsion. One ship was powered by steam driving two side-wheel paddle wheels; the other had a steam powered propeller. The two ships were cabled together stern to stern and each then applied full power to the combination. The propeller-powered ship towed the paddle-powered ship backwards at about three knots, quickly ending the debate in favor of screw propellers.

The American Civil War was, or at least should have been, a turning point in military history. Prior to that war the combatants could usually plan to fight in much the same way their predecessors had fought in recent previous wars. While they might win or lose, neither the tactics nor the strategy of their enemy would differ much from recent wars. That is not to say that one side could not surprise the other but that surprise would almost always be within the scope of what military forces, both land and sea, had done in the recent past or could reasonably have been expected to do. In spite of the steady but exceedingly slow evolution of weapons both on land and sea, the military doctrines of the nineteenth century, especially with respect to land battles, slavishly followed the tactics of Wellington and Napoleon with respect to concentration of forces, slow movements of troops, use of artillery and often lack of concealment or protection. This was in spite of the increased range and accuracy of infantry weapons and the availability of exploding cannon shells to supplement the killing power of solid shot and canister (metal cans filled with bullets and fired from artillery pieces) used in some earlier battles. A few commanders on both sides of the American Civil War seemed to realize that new tactics were needed to deal with the different weapons then appearing in battle. The ideas of those free thinkers were generally ignored by most senior military commanders even up to World War I.

The gap between the progress in weapon design and the teaching in military academies should have been made clear by the tactics used by both sides in the American Civil War. In that war, charges were made by men usually walking in mass formations into cannon and small arms fire, sometimes with defenders being located in barricades or natural cover although the mechanics of reloading the arms of that era often made it difficult to do other than to fight standing upright in the open. The longer ranged shoulder weapons of the Civil War meant that charging infantry, in addition to receiving cannon fire, would have to accept several volleys of the longer range fire from small arms located in their objective without responding because it was impossible for them to reload their weapons while on the move. The defenders could fire into the chargers as often as they could reload from a stationary position. Nor was there much effort to spread the attacking formations out to make them more difficult targets since concentration of forces was a sacred tenet.

The battle casualties of that war were high compared to the number of men engaged, due in large measure to the use of Nepoleonic and Wellingtonian tactics in the face of far more effective weapons than either of those earlier commanders had ever faced. The North and South[18] combined casualty rate for battle deaths in the Civil War was usually felt to be about 7% of the combined armies as opposed to a similar rate for American troops in World War I of a little over 1%. World War I figures for the United States are not directly comparable to the Civil War numbers given the relatively short time the United States was involved in battles in World War I (roughly one-fifth of the time in battles as was the case in the Civil War). If one multiplied the actual World War I casualty rates by the difference in the length of time

---

18 The South's rate for all causes of death was considerably higher than that of the North. It is sometimes claimed that one-quarter of the Southern white men of military age died in the Civil War. This is possible but not likely. Approximately 130,000 Southern soldiers died in the war. That was about 25% of the lowest estimate of the total number of Southern troops but was 9% of the highest estimate and in either case makes the unlikely assumption that all those white males of military age were wearing Confederate uniforms.

of combat, the loss rates in World War I would be approximately the same as those of the Civil War. The disconnect between new weapons and old tactics was not only ignored in the Civil War, it continued to be ignored throughout World War I. Because of the much greater percentage of the male population of the North and South involved in the Civil War as contrasted to the percentage involved in World War I, the result was that the combined casualty lists in that war looked rather similar although when applied to the population figures in the second decade of the twentieth century the death rate in the Civil War was approximately five times that of World War I even after adjusting that rate for time in battle. Again the types of charges used were largely those of 100 years earlier – men charging across open ground. But by 1914 the machine gun had been perfected and produced in great numbers. Rifles had far greater range and accuracy combined with a much higher rate of fire as a result of magazines containing five to eight rounds which could be reloaded while the soldier was under cover or on the move. The result was even more slaughter on the battlefield. That is without taking into account the casualties from newer sources of mayhem such as more effective artillery, attacking aircraft, poison gas, mortars and barbed wire. This lack of appreciation in Europe of the changes in warfare from the Napoleonic era to World War I is particularly surprising in light of the number of military observers from European countries who were present in the United States during the Civil War and who saw first hand many of the bloody battles. It should also be mentioned that in both wars the American deaths from non-battle causes (mainly accidents and illness) were greater than those from battle.

By the very end of the Civil War the machine gun (in the form of the Gatling gun) had become a factor, although quite minor, on those battlefields. Somewhat ironically Dr. Gatling had invented his early form of machine gun, patented in 1861, in the hope that it would be so deadly that it would discourage war. He was quite correct about its killing power but very wrong about the reaction to it. While not a factor in the Civil War, by the end of that war a Prussian shoulder weapon, the needle gun,[19] had been invented and used with great effect in European wars from 1864 to 1871. That gun made infantry more mobile but also made cavalry much more vulnerable as the infantry then had the ability to fire more shots at longer range at such large targets

Before we consider the remarkable pace of development of weapons beginning in the mid-nineteenth century it is important to keep in mind the difference between an arms race and an armaments race. An arms race is quantitative; an armament race is qualitative. In its simplest form an arms race pits the contestants against each other with more or less similar equipment, the assumption being that, all other factors being equal, the side with the most troops and the most equipment would have the advantage and should win the battle. It would probably be a battle of logistics if the quantity and quality of the troops or ships were reasonably similar. There is an old adage among professional soldiers to the effect that amateurs worry about tactics; professionals worry about logistics. These old rules of battle still serve well.[20] An armament race is an effort to develop and put into place markedly different and more effective weapons than the enemy has available at the time. The use of such better weapons should confer a significant if not determinative advantage on their users. Generally omitted from the subject of armament races are the products of brilliant historical figures whose contributions may have been very great but much of whose work is not able to be judged objectively for lack of solid information. Archimedes and Leonardo da Vinci, among others, would fit into this category. It would be most interesting to know who invented the great naval armament known as "Greek fire" sometime in

---

19 Called such because it used a needle-shaped firing pin in a musket/rifle. The needle pierced the paper cartridge and struck a detonator which ignited the powder. The result was that paper cartridges could be used effectively, allowing for faster loading in any firing position.

20 Those tactics could often be quite simple. General Nathan Bedford Forest, CSA, described them as "Get there first with the most men." While Bartlett, *Familiar Quotations* (14th ed. 1968), p. 709b, cites this language as correct, it points out that the statement is usually but erroneously quoted as "Git thar fustest with the mostest."

the middle of the first millennium C.E. and exactly what it was made of, when it was first used and how it was used.

In contrast to the relative inaction of armies to even some minor evolutions of weapons, the navies of the world evolved considerably in the mid-nineteenth century and it was in those navies at that time that we begin to see the point-counterpoint of rapid weapon development and armament races that prevailed for the next century and a half.

While historically new naval weapons and tactics had been eventually countered to some degree, the reaction had usually been much belated and piecemeal. As suggested above, in 1859 different and important approaches to naval battles begin to appear sporadically and new weapons seemed to call for other and better weapons to become available more rapidly. These first appeared in two events very closely connected in time but not in place or context. The first event was the decision of the French navy to build an armored battleship. It would be the first armored ship at least in the Western world although there is some evidence that the Chinese had armored at least one large junk several centuries earlier. The French Navy built *La Gloire*, a small and not very handsome battleship (sometimes listed as an armored frigate), which had used an earlier battleship design cut down by one deck, presumably to provide the additional buoyancy necessary to offset the weight of the iron. She was constructed in the usual wooden ship manner and then had four-inch thick iron plates fastened to the hull from the waterline to the rail. Two sister ships, *Invincible* and *Normandie*, followed in short order. The Royal Navy responded to the challenge quite promptly. While the French and the British had recently cooperated against the Russians in the Crimean War, they had generally been at each others' throats for the preceding 600 years. Thus the Royal Navy was deeply concerned that the French navy had produced a heavy vessel that might be invulnerable to the weapons with which the Royal Navy had then equipped its fleet. Its wariness was increased by its competition with the French for African colonies, competition with many nations for Pacific islands and ongoing Caribbean disputes. The immediate response from the British was to build a better armored ship which they did and quickly enough to have her completed in 1860. She was named HMS *Warrior* and had a hull of armor built over a wooden framework. In contrast to *La Gloire, Warrior* was a handsome ship.

Both ships were sail powered with steam as an auxiliary power source. Because *Warrior* had all of her main armament on one deck, under the ancient rules of the Admiralty she was labeled a frigate and not a battleship (or a ship-of-the-line). Normally frigates were much weaker vessels than battleships but that was certainly not the case with *Warrior*. Neither ship ever fired her guns in anger. *La Gloire* and her sister ships were scrapped earlier than planned when their wooden hulls rotted. *Warrior* and her sister ship, HMS *Black Prince,* served longer but were eventually decommissioned and *Warrior* was lost track of, only to be rediscovered much later as a store ship in a busy English port. Under the patronage of the Duke of Edinburgh she was restored and is now on display in Portsmouth. In spite of the lack of action against each other, the major technical advance of *La Gloire* and the prompt response of *Warrior* is probably the first instance of what became over the next 150 years normal, rapid, expensive and dangerous armament races. As it turned out, the British had little to fear from the French in this period. France's defeat by Prussia in 1870-71, the creation of modern Germany from Prussia and other smaller German states and the powerful German economy eventually directed France away from its large warship race with its historic enemy and toward protecting itself on the ground from its nearby expanding neighbor to the east.

While *La Gloire* won the armament race as the first armored naval ship it was a very short-lived advantage which the French did not attempt to exploit during the year before *Warrior* appeared to end the armament race and to introduce an arms race for battleships which the Royal Navy was to win easily.

It is a curious coincidence that the next rapid thrust and parry of complicated weapons occurred only two years later than the *La Gloire-Warrior* developments after centuries of such major events in the past occurring many decades apart.[21] These next events involved the naval departments of the Union and the Confederacy. In the Civil War the North had, early on, undertaken to blockade the Southern ports in order to prevent the export of Southern corps such as tobacco and cotton and to block the import of military material, mostly purchased with the proceeds of the sale of the tobacco and cotton. The South had some fast ships able to act as blockade runners but those ships did not have enough carrying capacity for the South's needs. The South therefore had to find a way to destroy the Union blockade, particularly in Chesapeake Bay. By sheer chance early in the war there fell into the hands of the South a partially burned Union ship, USS *Merrimack.* The hulk was located very conveniently in Chesapeake Bay. The South planned to rebuild her as a mastless ironclad steam vessel of very slow speed and short cruising range but with a powerful cannon battery. The ship, soon to be renamed CSS *Virginia,* could have caused havoc among the unarmored vessels comprising the Union blockading fleet in the restricted waters of the bay. The South did not have the infrastructure to do the reconstruction quickly and knowledge of what was afoot soon reached the North.[22] This of course caused the North to try to speed up the completion of its revolutionary iron, armored, steam-driven, mastless ship equipped with a steam-powered turret containing two very powerful cannons. A quite unusual looking ship resulted described by one observer as "a cheese box on a raft." She was named USS *Monitor* and gave her name to a class of ships which, in spite of their enclosed heavy batteries or perhaps because of them, had poor sea-keeping qualities. By an extraordinary quirk of fate *Monitor* reached the Chesapeake the day after *Virginia* had started her destruction of the Northern blockading fleet. The two ironclads spent the day of *Monitor's* arrival hammering at each other with solid

---

21 Some idea of the lack of evolution in naval vessels in that era is shown by the fact that HMS *Victory,* Admiral Nelson's flagship at Trafalgar, was 40 years old at the time of the battle.

22 The amount of information and commerce that passed between the two combatants was astounding, including Southern military uniform buttons manufactured in a Connecticut factory and Southern currency printed in New York.

shot without serious harm being done to either vessel.[23] Nevertheless, when *Virginia* left the bay in order to return to her base, the old rule for land engagements, that possession of the battlefield equals victory, was asserted at sea by *Monitor*. *Virginia* left her mark on naval design in a rather unexpected way. A number of Union gunboats built later in the war and used generally on rivers owed their design in large measure to *Virginia*.

Technically one might say that the South won the armament race with a solely stream powered, armored and all big gun vessel but that advantage was lost 24 hours later. In the subsequent arms race there was no contest. The North built a number of Monitors during and after the Civil War.

The combined developments of *Warrior* and *Monitor* made virtually all heavy ships of the navies of the world not just obsolete but worthless in conflict with ironclad ships, an event that was to have an eerie and very important parallel in Britain in 1906. After the Civil War the United States Navy produced a number of Monitors in both single and dual turret versions but otherwise the designers reverted to sails and wooden hulls with steam power as a mere auxiliary. Its principal reason for that approach was that the major concern of the United States Navy was harbor defense for which the Monitors were well suited and that sailing ships could show the flag around the world more cheaply than steam-powered ships. Secondary reasons were that the Monitors would have had to be redesigned both to be carry enough coal for long distance cruising and to provide the much greater freeboard required for ocean travel. For a part of the rest of the century, the British and the French were building battleships intended to fight each other in accordance with their historical practice. Their ships had varying armor, speed,

---

23 The designer of *Monitor* was outraged that only solid shot was used by her in the engagement. He had apparently assumed, quite correctly, that *Virginia*'s armor only ran down to her fully-laden waterline. As she used coal and shot during her battle with *Monitor* she became much lighter and thus exposed her vulnerable wooden hull which might have been badly damaged by the large exploding shells that *Monitor* could have fired.

seaworthiness, maneuverability, armament (size, number and position of their big guns) and displacement. But soon the European geopolitical world was to change as a result of the Prussian victories over Austria and France and the creation of the Second Reich, Germany.

The French and the English (British after the eighteenth century) initially had been at odds for hundreds of years. After 1066 when the Normans from France conquered England there was peace between the two countries for several centuries. Thereafter the descendants of the French invaders were often at war with their distant, both in geography and relationship, relatives. From the Hundred Years War (over who owned large sections of France) won by France and the Thirty Years War (when England became Protestant while France stayed Roman Catholic) through other continental wars culminating with two decades of war between the United Kingdom and Napoleon's France, Britain and France were often at war. These wars were fought on the continent of Europe or at sea and never reached the British Isles with the minor exception of a brief and unsuccessful French expedition into Ireland. The two nations were also fierce competitors for colonial empires but France usually came in second in those competitions, as was the case in Canada, India and several islands in the Caribbean. In most of the nineteenth century not only were there no direct conflicts between these long-time enemies, they actually cooperated in the Crimean War which pitted Turkey, France and Great Britain against Russia. Notwithstanding this Britain and France remained competitors, at least commercially, although France also tried to keep up with the Royal Navy for at least a some years in the ironclad era. In 1870-71 France was soundly defeated by Prussia, losing two important provinces in the process. Prussia then transmuted itself into Germany by adding some additional Germanic provinces, becoming even more powerful thereby. France continued for a few years to some degree to compete with Britain in vessel design and construction but eventually gave up trying in order to concentrate on building up its army to prepare for another war with the increasingly powerful German army and that of its not quite so powerful ally, Austria-Hungary. On the other hand, the Prussian navy had been so inconsequential that the first commander of the German navy was an army general. In due course the situation was improved by putting an admiral in command and beginning a substantial shipbuilding program. In that era a battleship was the most important ship in any fleet. The number of battleships in a country's navy was a rough indication of the strength of that navy. By 1900 the German navy had about one-eighth the number of battleships in the Royal Navy. Even recognizing that the Royal Navy had many obligations around the world which required the presence of some of the ships of the navy, in its home waters it was still of overwhelming power.

By the end of the century the French had finally dropped the pretense of trying to maintain any sort of parity with the Royal Navy in the numbers and effectiveness of heavy vessels. Instead they turned their attention to their land forces and their probable confrontation with the emerging ever more powerful war machine of Germany. This left Great Britain for a time in control of most of the world's oceans. The absence of complete control showed up occasionally, as was the case in Samoa. In the eighteen nineties Great Britain, the United States and Germany (but not France) were competing for the ability to establish coaling facilities for their ships in the Samoan Islands to service their commercial activities as well as their navies. Each of the three countries supported a separate Samoan group in an eight-year civil war that almost included a naval battle among the three western nations. Fortunately a large and timely storm developed in the area, scattering and damaging the fleets and thus largely defusing most aspects of the matter. In 1899 a treaty was signed giving Germany a large portion of the Samoan Islands, the United States a smaller portion and Great Britain none. In the long run this made little difference, particularly since at the end of World War I the British Empire acquired the German interests in Samoa as war booty. It does, however, indicate how much Germany and the United States had risen in naval matters and how far France had fallen.

The *Dreadnought* Dilemma

During the last part of the nineteenth century there was certainly not an armament race among the navies of Great Britain, France, Germany, Russia and the United States – the ships were much too similar. There might have been an arms race but for the fact that no one could have won it except the Royal Navy. Since France had effectively dropped out of the naval side to concentrate on her army and Germany, Russia and the United States never started, Great Britain would already have been drinking tea at the finish line of any naval arms race. The United States was not interested in that kind of a race and, in 1900, Germany had about 15% as many battleships as Great Britain without much hope of gaining on the Royal Navy.[24] Then Great Britain in 1906 changed everything by building HMS *Dreadnought*, a completely new type of battleship which made all existing battleships as outmoded as wooden hulled sailing ships and causing Germany, and Great Britain, to have wasted their recently spent money on predreadnought battleships. Now a British instigated arms race was under way with the Americans competing in rather leisurely fashion and the Germans competing quite frantically to build Dreadnoughts. Initially each of those countries was only one or two Dreadnought battleships behind Britain.

Dreadnought was a dramatically new weapon for three reasons. She was equipped with steam turbine engines in place of the traditional reciprocating engines producing more speed and, perhaps more importantly, having much less maintenance on her engines. She had a central fire control system for all five of her turrets. Most importantly, her big guns were all of the same caliber. While this last innovation

---

24 This serious and probably uncorrectable German deficit in predreadnought battleships at that time did not deter the Germans from at least giving lip service to a substantial battleship building program. In 1901 Admiral von Tirpitz, the commander of the German navy, refused to spend much money on submarines in favor of spending more on battleships. Massie, *Castles of Steel* (2003), p. 126. The admiral was probably wrong.

might appear of only dubious value it was not. Prior to *Dreadnought* it was the practice to equip battleships with as many cannons as could be mounted. The result was guns of several different calibers depending on the amount of space that could be allocated to the guns and their related equipment and supplies. It had been felt for generations that the best way to fight a naval battle was to fire as much ammunition of all sizes as was possible at one's enemy but two recent wars had suggested that with modern big guns this had become an incorrect strategy.

When in the past naval battles had been fought at close range the gunners could see where their shots were hitting. As cannons were developed with longer range, it became necessary to find a way to spot the fall of shot and to correct the aim of the weapons appropriately. The method that was used was to place spotters high on the masts of firing ships to observe where their shots were landing and to send messages to the gunners below as to how they should adjust their aim. In reviewing the naval battles of the Spanish-American War in 1898 and of the Russo-Japanese War in 1904 it was determined that the spotter often could not tell the difference between, for example, the splash of a shell from an 8 inch gun and the splash of a shell from a 10 inch gun. The result of such confusion could be that the gun which needed to have its aim corrected would not be adjusted and the gun which had its aim changed in response to the spotter's report would thereby have been adjusted further off its target. The solution to this very serious gun laying problem was twofold. First, make all of the big guns on each ship identical in barrel diameter, barrel length and ammunition so that all the shells in the salvo would be following the same trajectory and second, have the big guns on every ship all aimed and fired by the same director. This should produce tight salvos, the splashes of which could be more easily identified by the spotter and corrected onto the target.

While the first design for a battleship of this type was created by an Italian naval architect, the Italian government felt that it would be too expensive to build such a ship.[25] The next country to consider

---

25 Somewhat surprisingly the cost turned out to be only about 20% more than that

the concept was the United States. The ships in a two-ship class of that design to be named USS *South Carolina* and USS *Michigan* were proposed to Congress in 1904. There being no particular naval emergency to hurry the matter along, the Congressional approval and appropriation process took until 1906 and construction of those two ships was not completed until 1910. Great Britain, for various reasons, was more anxious to build one of the new type of battleships named HMS *Dreadnought*, which was completed in 1906 after about only one year of construction.[26] It had been possible to build her so rapidly because most of her big guns were diverted from other battleship construction. The manufacture of main battery guns was the most time-consuming aspect of battleship and battle cruiser construction. In spite of some teething problems she was put into service promptly. Germany instantly realized that rather than being hopelessly far behind Great Britain in battleships, because all earlier battleships, British and German, were obsolete Germany was now only one ship behind. The Germans immediately started a building program as did the British. The situation changed from an armament race, briefly won by the British, to an arms race, the result of which was undetermined for eight years. The race included both battleships and battle cruisers built on the Dreadnought model.[27]

Although *Dreadnought* was actually built in about a year, even including the planning beginning with the publication of the concept a

---

of predreadnought battleships and the lower maintenance costs of the turbine engines in *Dreadnought* would probably have reduced the differential even further.

26 For a more complete discussion of the causes and consequences of the construction of *Dreadnought*, see Greer, *The First Decade of the Twentieth Century* (2004), pp. 72-100.

27 Battle cruisers were an odd concept. They carried the same size main armament guns as battleships although not necessarily the same number of guns, but they were a few knots faster by virtue of their lighter armor. That might have made sense except that both countries used battle cruisers as part of their battle lines, exposing their battle cruisers to the same punishment that was given to battleships without the battle cruisers having the protection of battleship armor. The results were entirely predictable.

total of less than four years was consumed in the conception, planning, designing and constructing of her. This was an extremely short time to produce something as large, as complex and as original as *Dreadnought*. It was a good example of a coming trend in armament races; short periods for concepts, plans, designs, construction and testing. If someone were particularly perspicacious he might have deduced this trend a half century earlier with the building of *Warrior* even though *Warrior*, in spite of her dramatic impact on large warship design, was a much simpler project. We shall see more of these types of hasty, sometimes reckless, leaps forward into uncharted technology during the remainder of the twentieth century. This approach sometimes produced good results and sometimes the opposite. In the case of *Dreadnought* the technical results were generally very good but the strategic concepts were not so simply judged.

It has never been quite clear why the British built *Dreadnought* when they did. They must have realized that by doing so they would lose their enormous lead in battleships over the Germans who, by then, had made it clear to the world that they would soon be on the conquest trail toward France and much of the rest of Europe combined. Perhaps the moving force for Britain was an effort to be certain to stay ahead of the rest of the world. The Royal Navy knew that the United States was well into the process of convincing Congress to authorize two of what would later be called Dreadnought-type battleships and that Germany had the idea of some sort of a Dreadnought ever since the Italian designer had published his design concepts. Since both of the United States and Germany had the industrial bases to build such ships fairly rapidly if they chose to do so, the British would not have wanted to fall behind either country. In the case of the United States Britain need not have worried for the United States took its time in building its first two Dreadnoughts. On the other hand, since Germany had moved so rapidly to follow the Royal Navy's lead in building *Dreadnought*, it would have been a reasonable precaution by the British to start early on their own accelerated construction program lest Germany built the first new battleships. The reason for the British move might also have been pure pride. That pride might have been pride of the Royal Navy in having the best battleship in the world or it might have been personal pride on the part of Admiral Fisher who, as the First Sea Lord (the senior officer in the Royal Navy), had invented part of what became *Dreadnought* although some of his ideas for the ship were rejected and others that were incorporated into the final version probably should not have been.

There was no question that Great Britain, with *Dreadnought*, had won the modern battleship armament race against Germany and the United States but, well before there were any naval actions involving battleships, the Germans had entered into perhaps the greatest arms race the world had ever seen to that date. Britain won that arms race but not overwhelmingly. The result of that race was catastrophic for many countries since it convinced the Germans that they were close enough to Britain in large naval vessels in service to have a chance to defeat the Royal Navy if war finally erupted between Great Britain and Germany. It may very well have been that by winning the armament race with HMS *Dreadnought* the British encouraged Germany to start World War I. That statement obviously requires some explanation. Had Britain left its huge battleship fleet alone in 1906, the year *Dreadnought* was built, Germany would not have gone to a crash program to build battleships and battle cruisers in the Dreadnought mode. The situation is an excellent example of what not to do with advanced weapons development. If one country (here Britain) has an overwhelming advantage in a category of weapons, that country must be very careful about outmoding that category for by so doing it would run a serious risk of outmoding its own forces while giving a potential enemy a chance to participate in an arms race with both countries at the starting line at about the same time. Certainly if one knows that the potential enemy will start down the same path there would be no harm and considerable advantage in getting an earlier start. Nevertheless, unless one is reasonably sure that the enemy will proceed down the same path, it is neither sensible nor cost efficient to make one's own arsenal obsolete.

World War I

The naval arms race continued into the beginning of World War I and the British had stayed a bit ahead of the Germans. The German strategy to deal with this disparity once the seemingly inevitable war had begun was to try to slip some of their heavy ships out of their bases into the North Sea to isolate and engage a few of the Royal Navy's capital ships. If the Germans were successful in finding and isolating a few of those ships and then sinking them, Germany might have a chance to reduce the Royal Navy's numerical advantage in Dreadnought type battleships, perhaps to something of a parity with Germany. In that case they felt that their better gun laying equipment and ship compartmentalization[28] would allow them to defeat some of the British battleships with little loss to Germany. That in turn would enable the misnamed German High Seas Fleet to attack the British Grand Fleet with a reasonable chance of defeating it. By defeating the Grand Fleet, Germany, with its submarines as well as surface vessels, would control the waters around the British Isles with all the consequences for the British that blockading their homeland would mean. It was not to be. The major confrontation of Dreadnoughts at the Battle of Jutland in 1916 ended in pretty much a draw. Although in the battle Great Britain lost more ships than Germany in the battle, the damaged British ships were repaired rapidly whereas the damaged German ships were under repair for months. The Germans abandoned the North Sea, at least for their battleships and battle cruisers, and returned to their harbors leaving control of the North Sea in the hands of the Royal Navy. Thus the naval arms race was won by the British after they had temporarily won the naval armament race.

---

28 Compartmentalization was important because the more compartments a ship had below the main deck the harder it was for an enemy to sink the ship but the more difficult it was for the crew get around the ship. The Germans did not plan to spend as much time at sea as the Royal Navy so they were not so concerned about the crew's comfort while at sea.

World War I produced a number of armament races. The French won the light artillery race with the remarkable French 75mm cannon. The British won the tank race by default. The Germans won the machine gun race, at least for the early part of the war, and the poison gas race for the whole war. By the end of the war the American Browning Automatic Rifle was the best light machine gun. In fact it was so good that it was widely used throughout World War II. The best manual rifle was rather a tossup, with German Mauser bolt-action being the class of rifle bolt actions while the American 1903 Springfield was the most accurate rifle, particularly in the hands of United States Marines who were trained to shoot at very distant targets.

The arms race with submarines was especially serious. At the beginning of the war both Great Britain and Germany had produced operational submarines in some quantity, with the French and Austro-Hungarian navies a bit behind.[29] There were a few individual submarine missions of considerable importance early in the war, including the sinking of three Royal Navy cruisers in one hour by a German submarine, but the true value, or risk, depending on which side one was on, was in commerce raiding by German submarines especially on merchant traffic and troop transports en route across the Atlantic Ocean to the British Isles. The reason such small and slow vessels were so dangerous was their principal weapon, the torpedo. By the time of World War I the torpedo had evolved from a waterborne stationary mine in the American Civil War[30] to a self-propelled underwater weapon. It was particularly dangerous to vessels, both naval and civilian, because not only did it carry a very powerful warhead but also the torpedo exploded underwater

---

29 It was not generally appreciated that perhaps the best submarine captain in the Austro-Hungarian navy during World War I was an Austrian, Baron von Trapp of the singing family. See generally von Trapp, *To the Last Salute* (Campbell translation) (2007). His rapid departure with his family from Austria was occasioned by the *Reichsmarine*'s ordering him to Germany after the *Anschluss* gave Germany control over Austria in 1938.

30 Which explains Admiral Farragut's famous order at the Battle of Mobile Bay when he was warned of torpedoes (anchored mines) in the harbor - "Damn the torpedoes, full speed ahead."

against the hulls of its targets. The water contained much of the force of the explosion which would otherwise have been dissipated into the air, thus producing more damage than a similar weight of explosives would cause if delivered by cannon shells. Furthermore the torpedo damage would be under water and thus more dangerous to its target.[31]

Submarines were very elusive weapons. Not only could they attack without warning from beneath the water, they could submerge to avoid detection. This type of escape was much easier for them in World War I than in World War II. In World War II there were three separate ways to find and track submarines; if the submarine were on the surface (where submarines of that era spent the vast majority of their time) by radar, if it were submerged by sonar from surface ships which sent out signals under water that reflected back to the surface ship and by passive hydrophones which allowed surface ships to listen for the sounds of submerged submarines. In World War I only the last procedure was available and it could often be avoided by the submarine simply by shutting down its engines. Although the risk of strangulation of British trade made the U-boats in the Atlantic Ocean potentially very dangerous foes even in World War I, it was that same activity, expanded to submarines sinking noncombatant vessels, that drove the United States to enter into the war on the Allied side. The German winning of the arms race in submarine construction and use was thus a double-edged sword. It was the entry of the United States and its fresh troops that began to stream into Europe in 1918 that broke the deadlock in France and forced the Germans to surrender before the Allies were able to drive into Germany itself. In the twenties and thirties the Nazis claimed that the war had been lost not in battle but rather by revolutionary forces and disaffected starving civilians in Germany. In fact in September of 1918 the German General Staff sent the second highest ranking officer in the German army to Berlin to tell the government to make peace with the Allies quickly because the German army could no longer stop the Allied drive to the east.

---

31 This advantage is often described as "if you want to let air into an enemy ship fire shells; if you want to let water in use torpedoes."

One related series of armament races in World War I captured the public's attention beyond all others. They arose in connection with the introduction of a new weapon into warfare. It was not that those armament races had a great impact on the course of the war. Nor did they produce large casualty lists. They did, however, generate an enormous amount of publicity. These, of course, were the aviators and their machines.

While aircraft had been used in a very limited way in a few earlier minor wars, World War I was the first war in which aviation had played any significant part. The contribution of aircraft to the war was at first miniscule since the available aircraft could hardly get into the air and if they did they were only used for observation purposes. Initially there were no weapons designed to shoot down the observation planes with fire from the ground and enemy observation aircraft were not armed. The pilots of the adversaries, when meeting in the air, would usually simply wave to each other. Of course war was war and, after it was realized that even the observation aircraft pilots were enemies and not simply part of an international fraternity of aviators, efforts were made on the ground to try to shoot enemy planes down. Antiaircraft guns were developed. The concept of using specialized machine guns capable of firing upwards toward aircraft resulted in a rather cumbersome mounting for such guns. A post was driven vertically into the ground. A wagon wheel was attached horizontally to the top of the post and allowed to rotate freely. A machine gun was attached to the rim of the wheel. The gun itself could pivot vertically. The combination of these two motions would, in theory, allow the machine gun to follow the flight of an enemy aircraft. In practice, however, it proved very difficult to track the aircraft with the gun, particularly if the planes were flying directly over the gun. A second type of antiaircraft weapon was a ground-based cannon firing shells with timed fuses. The time of the fuses could be set to explode the shells when it was thought that the shells would be near the target aircraft. Enemy aircraft, however low, slow and fragile, were not in much danger from either type of antiaircraft fire during the early stages of the war.

The second method of an army attempting to destroy enemy aircraft observing over its territory was to have one of its aircraft try to shoot down the observer. This was a concept that developed slowly. After the initial period of non-aggression between aircraft of otherwise warring nations, armed conflict began. In the beginning the conflict involved only pistol and rifle shots between planes. This activity might have given some comfort to the combatants in that they seemed to be doing something although the short range of pistols and the windage created by the movement of the planes in flight made hitting one's target very unlikely. Gradually all parties came to understand that installing machine guns in aircraft was necessary if one were going to bring down enemy aircraft and that the best way to fire machine guns at another aircraft was to fasten the machine guns in the pursuing aircraft pointing forward and then aiming the aircraft, not the guns, at the target.[32] It worked well with pusher-type aircraft because their engine and propeller were at the back of the fuselage, leaving a clear field of fire for the machine gun mounted forward. This would have been an excellent solution except that pusher-powered aircraft of that era did not work as well as their tractor-powered equivalents. It would have been possible to mount a machine gun in front of the pilot firing forward on a tractor-powered fighter but for the propeller. If the gun were positioned to fire forward from anywhere on the fuselage of the plane, that gun position would cause the bullets to enter the arc of the wooden propeller and damage the blades. An effort was made to put armor on the blades to deflect the bullets but that did not work well. Since the construction of fighters in those days was very light to enable the weak engines available to power the fighters to as high a performance level as possible, it was not structurally possible to mount a heavy machine gun or, preferably for balance purposes, a pair of machine guns, one on each wing, to fire outside of the propeller arc without materially degrading the plane's performance by the weight of additional wing structure and an additional machinegun. This left, as the only place to mount a gun that would fire straight ahead and be solidly mounted, the center of the top wing, most World War I fighter

---

32 It is not generally appreciated except by experienced combat pilots how much the reaction of forward-firing weapons reduced the speed of the firing aircraft.

aircraft being biplanes This location kept the bullets out of the way of the propeller blades, it did not require the weight of two guns to keep the plane balanced and it gave the pilot a rough idea of where the bullets were going. The disadvantages of this arrangement were two. First the pilot did not have an accurate gunsight right in front of his face so aiming was both inconvenient and inaccurate. Second, since the aircraft-mounted machine guns of that period were prone to jamming problems, having the gun so far from to the pilot prevented him from clearing jams unless he stood up in the cockpit. This was neither safe nor convenient in the course of an air battle, to say nothing of the information about the status of his machine gun that would thus be conveyed to any of his enemies within sight of him, attracting unwanted attention during his defenseless period.

It was during the time when pilots began to try to kill each other that the newspapers started to popularize the aviators, particularly the fighter pilots. They were analogized to eagles, they were the modern equivalents of the medieval knights errant searching the world for the enemies of their masters, and they were considered supermen of a sort because of their ability to able to operate one of the most modern, complicated and dangerous, to friend and foe alike, weapons of the war. For the remainder of the war the aviators received publicity far beyond what they deserved based upon their contributions to the war effort but perhaps it was warranted because of the extreme danger of their profession.

In 1915 a new and very effective German fighter aircraft appeared over the battlefields of France. It was the tractor-powered Fokker Eindecker 1, a monoplane as its name indicated. The big surprise was not that it was a monoplane at a time when biplanes were the rule but was rather that it had a forward firing machine gun mounted on the top of the fuselage directly in front of the pilot. For a while there was some mystery about why this aircraft did not shoot off its own propeller in battle but eventually examination of an E1's wreckage showed that Fokker had invented a device, usually called an interrupter, which prevented the gun from firing at times when a propeller blade would have been hit by a bullet. This obviously reduced the rate of fire of the gun somewhat but the fact that the period was called the Fokker Scourge indicates strongly that the E1 did very well against both the British Newport (a conventionally armed tractor powered biplane) and some rear engine fighters in the half year until the Royal Air Force and the Armee d'lAir caught up with the Fokker secret and installed it in their tractor-type aircraft. The Fokker E1 was such a departure from previous aircraft that it could be crowned as the winner of the fighter aircraft armament race. In spite of the short time needed to develop the interrupter system, the term Fokker Scourge applied to the E1 indicates just how important that system was. The fact that the Allies managed to copy the system in short order limited the effect of the interrupter system advantage to the Germans and returned the armament race to an arms race.

Fokker's next success was not as dramatic an improvement as that of the Eindecker but it quickly became better known to the public both within and without Germany. In 1917 the Fokker company developed another outstanding fighter. This time it was a more a copied response to a British step forward in fighter design than a completely new concept. In many respects the degree of some types of maneuvers that fighters can perform is a function of the surface area of the plane's wings. As a broad generalization, the more surface the more lift. To try to increase the wing area to increase the lift and therefore to improve maneuverability, wings could be made longer but that would require much stronger wing structures increasing the weight, reducing the maneuverability and increasing the drag thereby reducing speed. The wing could be made broader but there as well were structural and aerodynamic concerns plus a significant reduction in the pilot's visibility. The visibility available to a fighter pilot in World War I was critical to his survival. The final possibility, at least given the state of the art of aerodynamics at the time, was to add another wing and shorten the length of all wings. The British came up with idea first in the Sopwith Triplane which had, as expected, great maneuverability. Because of the increased frontal area of three wings and the associated drag, the top speed of the plane was relatively low. Nevertheless the combination of three wings and shorter wingspan made the Sopwith Triplane a good match for the German fighters in service at the time. The Germans then turned to their excellent aviation industry for a response in the best tradition of an armament race. A number of candidates were submitted and, after testing, the Fokker Dreidecker 1 (although designed by Reinhold Platz, Fokker's chief designer) was selected for service in one group of squadrons. It went into squadron service in 1917.

Baron von Richthofen, who downed 80 Allied aircraft before he was killed, made over a quarter of his victories in the Fokker D1. The plane was indeed an excellent dogfighter but it had two serious weak points. Like all triplanes it was slow, allowing enemy pilots who were reluctant to tangle with a D1 to avoid combat. That sort of avoiding conflict was then considered cowardly in contrast to present fighter combat concept that a pilot who finds himself at a tactical disadvantage should get out of the combat if at all possible. The World War I approach was particularly heroic since the pilots did not, as a rule, wear parachutes. The second serious problem with the D1 was its weak structure. After two early crashes due to structural failures, the planes were grounded to try to correct the problems and some progress was made. The exigencies of war at the time, however, required the planes to be put back into squadron service before all of the structural problems were resolved. Those failures caused continual nagging doubts about the plane because, as every pilot knows, there is not much one can do about structural failure in flight. While many of the problems were due to faulty construction, some shedding of wings was apparently the result of other causes. Well after the war when more had become known about aerodynamics, it was discovered that the differential lifting of the three wings tended to tear the plane apart. Some planes actually came safely back from non-combat flights missing their top wing if the pilot had been lucky enough to have had his top wing separate cleanly from the rest of the craft. The Fokker D1 was a successful aircraft and received a great deal of publicity on both sides of the war, in some measure due to the fame of certain of its pilots. It warranted the title of the winner of an armament race although its impact was not as great as that of either the E1 before it or the Fokker D.VII after it.

The next, and last, Fokker fighter in World War I was the Fokker D.VII (also designed by Paltz) which turned out be the best fighter of the war in any air force. It went into service in 1918 and was conventional in design, having a biplane configuration with a tractor engine and two machine guns firing through the propeller. It was docile with no bad habits in maneuvers, in contrast to most World War I fighters. It was so much better than its competitors that its destruction of enemy aircraft was known as the Second Fokker Scourge. It did, however, have a few problems. The wings tended to fail on occasion, the fuel tanks leaked and the ammunition storage was dangerous. Efforts were made to correct these faults but Germany's war effort was in dire straits by then and this plane too was put back in service without finding solutions to all of its problems. In spite of those problems the aircraft was sufficiently dangerous to its opponents to require a great and not successful effort on the part of Germany's enemies just to try to match the German planes. The D.VII was the only German airplane considered dangerous enough to be dealt with specifically in the war-ending documents. The D.VIIs were all taken from Germany after the war and given to other countries or destroyed. The D.VII might have been the winner of the last fighter aircraft armament race in World War I although it is not clear whether its preeminence was simply due to an excellent combination of previously known and used ideas.

The saga of the three Fokkers is a good example of armament races on a small scale. They were so far ahead of their contemporaries that combat with them was very difficult and their contemporaries were forced to dramatic efforts to try to create effective responses. There were two reasons why these aircraft were not war-deciding developments notwithstanding their advantages. First, the air war was a sideshow and a minor one at that;[33] the most important theaters of the war were the ground actions in France and the German

---

33 After stating that "[t]he First World War was the crucible of military aviation" the authors go on to say that "the Germans by their own count sustained no fewer that 1,200 air raids on the Western Front during the war, with 650 (mostly daylight) raids taking place in 1918. Actual damage to German war potential was negligible. . . " Caldwell & Muller, *The Luftwaffe over Germany* (2007), p. 14.

submarine attacks on the troops, military supplies and civilian food coming into Great Britain. Even had the Allies had lost the air war they certainly would not, as a result, have lost the ground war or suffered from the cutting of the supply line into Britain. Second, because of the simplicity of the design and construction of those aircraft, the response times of the Allies to react to major German advances in the air war were generally not only measured in months, they were measured in periods of a few months so the advantages of dramatic advances by either side in these areas were limited to brief periods, in most cases for only a few months. The one exception to this record was the Fokker D.VII in the last few months of the war. The war ended before the Allies had a chance to try to duplicate the performance of the Fokker. Whether they could have done so in any reasonable time is uncertain. It is important to note just how brief a time it took the warring nations to react to improved enemy fighter aircraft at least in these important instances. The reactions were a matter of a few months which included developing the concept, doing the planning, building the prototypes and conducting the test flights. It was a case of the exigencies of war coupled with the ease of aircraft construction that permitted this type of speed in such emergencies.

Four other categories of aviation activity in World War I should be discussed from the point of view of armament and arms races. The first two, bombing and observation aircraft, were used extensively by all of the combatants but the changes in them during course of the war by all participants, while significant, were not of the overwhelming nature of some of the fighter changes. There were another two categories of flying equipment that were important but they too did not have many modifications during the war. The first was that of anchored observation balloons. These were tethered to the ground close behind the front lines, filled with highly inflammable hydrogen and sent aloft with observer or two equipped with a telephone to the ground and parachutes. The observers, at least in daylight hours during good weather, would keep watch on enemy activity behind the front lines. This duty was quite hazardous because the observers were in a stationary, inflammable location and were easy prey for enemy fighters. To protect the balloons anti-aircraft guns were usually positioned near each balloon. If enemy fighters were sighted, the observers would call to the ground crew to crank the balloon down. Often the fighters came within firing range of the balloons before they reached the ground in which case the on-board observers parachuted down. The activity was not without danger from the fighter pilot's point of view either. The anti-aircraft fire was at very close range and a large cloud of burning hydrogen was not a pleasant thing to fly through. In fact, for some purposes fighter pilots received the same credit for destroying a passive observation balloon as for shooting down an enemy fighter. Nevertheless the use of observation balloons for military purposes dates back to the American Civil War so they were not a new idea for World War I. The equipment was simply updated.

The last category of World War I flying machines to be discussed was indeed new to warfare (although not to aviation) and was very frightening to its opponents. The dirigible was also a hydrogen filled container for flying but it differed from balloons in that it had an aluminum framework to shape the hydrogen container, engines to move it and moveable control surfaces to direct it. The basic plan of the dirigible had been developed before the war and had been perfected by Count von Zeppelin, a German general. His machines were huge, over 650 feet long with large crews, and were capable of reaching altitudes as high as 17,000 feet or more for long distances. They could also be equipped with defensive machine guns. The German dirigibles were called Zeppelins in honor of their builder and were primarily intended to bomb England. The British not only had nothing comparable to the Zeppelins, they had little to combat this victor of an armament race, at least initially. Soon various techniques were developed to try to destroy Zeppelins, including bombing them from above. Bombing from above had the usual problem of aiming the bomb to hit a large but moving target. The biggest problem, however, was usually trying to climb above the target Zeppelins which often operated at or about altitudes about at the maximum height the fighters could reach. The fighters' rate of climb at the Zeppelins' usual altitude would be very slow if they could even reach that height where the thin air made maneuvering to attack the Zeppelins very difficult. Most of the Zeppelins built for war service were destroyed, about equally by enemy action and by operational accidents. Zeppelins had a value as a terror weapon in the bombing of England although as it turned out not enough to justify their costs. One particular bombing tactic must have been very troublesome to the English. Zeppelins could into fly into the bottom of an overcast so they could not be seen even though the noise of their engines could be clearly heard on the ground. Their bombing would be directed by a crewmember who would be lowered in a small gondola to just below the overcast. It must have been quite nerve-racking to the crew member in the gondola when the British fighters came up and he was the only enemy target in sight. The Zeppelin crew would have to do some fast cranking to draw him back into the clouds before the British fighters reached him. Although the British did not find effective ways to stop the activities of the Zeppelins that turned out not to be crucial because the Zeppelins, while a new and potentially dangerous weapon, were not much of a danger to the Allies at that stage of their development. They were later abandoned by the Germans as not being cost-effective for further use. Curiously, the United States found blimps[34] very helpful in World War II, using their long range and slow speed to help to defend Atlantic Ocean convoys from German submarines.

If we examine the weapons and casualties of World War I we see that most of the killing was done by the same types of weapons used in most past wars, rifles, machine guns and artillery. Other than aircraft the most important new weapons were poison gas and tanks. Poison gas was an important German weapon developed by the great German

---

34 A blimp is a lighter-than-air craft somewhat like a dirigible without the metal stiffening. The United States controlled most of the world's supply of helium, a lighter-than-air gas but heavier than hydrogen. Thus the United States had a great advantage in all lighter-than-air craft. Although helium has less lifting power than hydrogen, it does not burn or explode.

chemist Fritz Haber.[35] It killed or wounded large numbers of Allied soldiers. The Allies did not often retaliate because they did not have some of the necessary poison gas science and because poison gas was much more dangerous to an advancing army than to a retreating enemy. The gas was heavier than air in order to keep it close to the ground where the enemy soldiers were. The gas not only settled near the ground, it filled shell holes, killing advancing soldiers taking shelter in the holes. This was thus an armament race which the Germans won, to some degree because the Allies declined in large measure to participate in it, not so much on ethical grounds as on the practical basis that they did not have the science to do it well. Also its use went counter not so much to the Allies ethics but as to their war plan. Not doing it well created an extreme risk to one's own troops. Tanks were another matter. The British won the armament race by building two models of similar tanks. These tanks, while very slow, were quite useful but were not determinative to the outcome of the war. By that late in the war the Germans were hard pressed to keep up with the current needs of the army. Using assets and talent at that time on a new scheme like tanks was not really feasible although several large German prototype tanks were built.

---

35 Who won a Nobel prize in 1918 but for chemistry (a way to produce ammonia), not a Nobel peace prize. One of the major uses of the ammonia so produced was in the manufacture of munitions.

Interbellum

World War I ended in November of 1918. It had been called the "War to End All Wars" and most people seemed to accept that title as a conclusion rather than as an objective. It was easy enough for the defeated to disarm or be disarmed as necessary, but the winners, Great Britain, France, the United States, Italy and Japan, were still armed. Great Britain, France, the United States and Italy were eager to disarm as rapidly as possible both to release the men who had been forced into military service and to reduce dramatically the enormous expense of keeping the huge military establishments that had been created for the war. Japan had not created large forces for the war nor did it participate very much but, notwithstanding that, it now found itself being presented with much of the German colonial empire in the Pacific. This largess was due not so much because of Japanese help to the Allied cause but rather was driven by British concerns that the United States, as the likely alternative donee of the German possessions and a major participant in the victory which had as yet received no tangible benefits for its wartime commercial and military activities, would receive them. If the United States had received those islands its presence in the Pacific between the wars would have been greatly enhanced, probably to the detriment of the British Empire. Unfortunately some of the German islands thus ceded to Japan had to be recaptured from the Japanese by the United States at great cost during World War II.

With respect to France, Great Britain and the United States, all were anxious, even desperate, to reduce the size of their military. They were also anxious to reduce their expenses for the development of new and improved weapons, particularly since they had large supplies of World War I weapons left with no likely enemies to use them on. There was thus no immediate pressure to manufacture or improve those weapons. With the downsized military and the huge supplies of rifles, machine guns, artillery of all sizes, ammunition of all types, naval ships of all descriptions and, most importantly for our purposes here, aircraft there was a many-year supply of virtually every type of weapon.

In the seemingly very remote possibility that another war loomed, it was generally felt that infantrymen could be trained and equipped quite quickly, weapons could be taken out of the cosmoline and other preservatives in which they would have been stored and made usable on short order and naval ships could be laid up in the meantime in a way that would permit them to be placed back in service fairly quickly. In contrast, aircraft could not easily be preserved because they were necessarily fragile and tended to be made of materials that were not intended to be stored or even to last very long in active service. After the end of the war the numbers of air crew members declined as much as those of the other services resulting in a large surplus of aircraft as compared to the flight and ground crew personnel still in uniform.

It is important to note that, by the end of World War I, there had been almost two-thirds of a century beginning with *La Gloire* in 1859 and ending with the end of World War I in 1918 in which the number of important weapons innovations increased dramatically. The times necessary to develop those major innovations were reduced equally dramatically in spite of the generally increasing complexity of those weapons. Equally impressive was the rapid response to these innovations by actual or potential adversaries. Armament races there were but the winners of those races often had little time to enjoy their advantages before those advantages were countered by equal or better weapons developed by their enemies. The record for a reaction in battle to an innovation remained, of course, the one-day spread between *Virginia* going into battle and *Monitor* arriving on the scene to counter her. That is not to say that the North reacted that quickly in the building race with *Virginia* but even there the reaction was a matter of only a few months to build a unique and complicated weapon.

After the conclusion of World War I there was little incentive for the armed forces of any country to spend the time and money on weapons to try to win an armament race. There were no enemies in view for those nations with the resources and the power to create new weapons. Gradually, as older weapons became unusable some new weapons were built as replacements. For most countries the first new weapons were aircraft for three reasons. First, aircraft in those days were relatively cheap to build. Second and perhaps most importantly, the leftover aircraft from World War I had deteriorated badly. Third because aircraft were so new the technology applicable to aircraft was evolving much faster than it was for other types of weapons.

Given the short time and little cost required to design and build an aircraft in those days, it would seem that the postwar period should have produced great innovations in aviation. It did not initially for several reasons. First with the huge surplus of aircraft of the Allies left over from the war and small postwar air forces, there were a great number of spare aircraft of the Allies from World War I and a much reduced need for them by their air forces. Since there were so many excess aircraft there seemed to be no need for new planes or even new designs. This approach in fact was used and might have made sense so long as there were no dangerous enemies in sight which had developing air forces and, more importantly, if the aircraft of that era, with wooden frames, cloth surfaces and exposed engines, did not deteriorate as fast as they did. The service life of the aircraft of that era was measured at most in months and often in weeks. The result was that, in four or five years after the war, the war surplus aircraft even if they had not been placed in service were almost worthless.[36] Yet the United States Army Air Corps, among other air services, was still flying them because it was somewhere between difficult and impossible to receive funding for replacements from Congress.[37] A related problem was what happened to some of those aircraft when they were flown. They crashed. This

---

36 It was this condition that gave rise to the court-marshal of General Mitchell, the head of the Army Air Corps, not for allowing the condition to arise but rather for publicizing the existence of the condition.

37 Perhaps the Air Corps should have used the approach that the Air Force used after World War II when it numbered a few new aircraft as later variations of obsolescent aircraft rather than entirely new aircraft. *e.g.*, the F-84F (Thunderstreak), the F-86D & F-86H (Sabres) and the F-94C (Starfire). The intent seemed to have been to mislead Congress into thinking that the appropriations requested were for minor improvements to existing aircraft rather than for the expenses of substantially new aircraft.

The author will continue his usual practice of listing an aircraft's nickname when the plane is first mentioned for the benefit of those readers who know United States military aircraft by their nicknames.

was more a problem for aircrew than for aircraft. Since there were so many surplus aircraft replacements were readably available; trained aircrew lost in crashes were simply not replaceable. Nevertheless the loss of both aircrew and aircraft continued until the mid-twenties when the Royal Air Force, the Armee d'lAir and the United States Army Air Corps began to think about a few new aircraft, both bombers and fighters (still being labeled as pursuits in the United States, a title that was not changed until after World War II).

The most important aircraft improvements, as has happened often, were initiated by new engine designs. In World War I most of the Allied fighters were powered by rotary engines because the power-to-weight ratio of those engines was very good for that era, an obviously important advantage for aircraft engines. The engines looked superficially somewhat like present day single bank radial aircraft engines. There were limits on the size of rotary engines so the weight of the aircraft was also limited accordingly, constraining the available strength of the planes structure, the amount of fuel and ordinance which could be carried and even the weight of the pilot. The rotary engines used in World War I bore no resemblance, physically or technically, to the rotary engines developed by Wankel after World War II. All references to rotary engines in this book will be to the World War I rotary. While it seems quite bizarre today, the engine and the propeller of rotaries were fastened together so that both of them rotated at the same speed. It is well beyond the scope of this book, and the ability of the author, to explain why the rotary engine had to rotate. What was important was that there were three major disadvantages to rotary engines. First, the rotation of the engine and the propeller together produced a great deal of torque, making turns by the aircraft against the torque difficult and turns with the torque tighter than usual. Second, the engine had a very limited throttle; it either ran at fixed speeds or stopped. Fortunately it came with a cut-off switch on the electrical system located in the cockpit. While taxiing the pilot would be kept busy switching the engine on and off to produce a decent average taxiing speed. Landing speeds were controlled in the same primitive manner. Third, there was a practical limit on the size of rotary engine of about 100 horsepower.

When more conventional gasoline powered aircraft engines, both redial and inline, were developed and made lighter, far more power became available, allowing the aircraft designers more freedom and the aircraft to be made larger, stronger and more heavily armed and armored.

When the United States started a post war rebuilding program to modernize its combat airpower, by coincidence a new system for identifying Army Air Corps aircraft had just been created. That system numbered each of the pursuits and the bombers sequentially. By looking just at those numbers one might conclude that great strides were being taken in the development of a more modern Air Corps. Between 1925 and 1930 there were 16 new pursuit aircraft and 9 new bombers designed by American companies and delivered to the Army Air Corps. One might reasonably assume that given all of those new models there would have been some developments that would have produced an armament race event. That assumption would be quite incorrect. There were some improvements and some disasters as well but a comparison between the P-1 (Hawk)[38] and the P-16, both biplanes, shows a total increase in maximum speed of about 10 miles per hour, an increase in fire power from one .50 and one .30 caliber machine guns to two .50 caliber and one .30 caliber machine guns (the latter in the back cockpit firing aft).[39] The XB-1 (Cyclops) bomber, a biplane, in 1925 carried a crew of five, two as gunners, at a top speed of 120 miles per hour with a bomb load of 2,500 pounds while the Y1B-9A bomber, a monoplane, in 1930 carried a crew of four, two as gunners, at a top speed of 188 miles per hour with a bomb load of 2,200 pounds. Although the speed of the Y1B-9A was significantly higher than that of the XB-1, it is important to note that, offsetting the speed differential, the earlier plane carried a bomb load of 300 pounds more and had one additional crewman.[40]

---

38   In this instance the nickname does not help much in identifying the model since the Curtiss P-1, the P-2, the P-3, the P-6 and the P-36 were all nicknamed Hawk and the P-5 (Superhawk) and the P-40 (Warhawk) were close. The P-16, also a Curtiss aircraft, did not receive a nickname for some reason.

39   Jones, *U.S. Fighters* (1975), pp. 1-3, 50.

40   Jones, *U.S. Bombers* (3rd edition 1980), pp. 11-13, 27-29.

The other formerly Allied armed forces were making roughly the same very slow progress in the development of aircraft but there as well were not dramatic changes that would confound a potential enemy by winning or even initiating an armament race. Notwithstanding the slow pace of aircraft development, the air arms of the former Allied powers were moving faster than their armies and navies in the creation and improvement of weapons. The armies were of course giving thought to the concept of tanks as initiated by the British Army during World War I but the rest of their hardware stayed largely as it had been in 1918. The navies were even less innovative, completing some construction initiated during the war but not doing much in most areas since the prevailing theory was that future major wars were not very likely. The two most active areas of naval development among the Allies, which seemed relatively insignificant in the twenties, were in aircraft carriers and submarines. German submarines in particular had shown during World War I that they could serve as very effective blockading vessels, a lesson that Germany demonstrated early in World War II that it had learned well. The other seeming minor area, aircraft carriers, had seen the beginnings of modern carrier construction toward the end of World War I. The Washington Naval Conference in 1921 treated aircraft carriers so cavalierly that the United States was able to exchange two partially built battle cruisers (USS *Lexington* and USS *Saratoga*), both of which had been in line for destruction under the conference's decisions, for the ability to convert them to fleet aircraft carriers. It, of course, did so very successfully to the great benefit of the United States Navy in World War II.

The United States was not the only country to take advantage of this possibility. Japan as well had two battle cruisers under construction and converted them to aircraft carriers. HIJMS *Akagi* and HIJMS *Kaga* were converted during the 1920s to large fleet carriers like *Lexington* and *Saratoga*. The conversion of the battle cruisers required some compromises in order to work around the design and construction already done. Those compromises seemed to have worked better for the Americans than for the Japanese based upon the abilities of those ships to take punishment from their enemies. The conversions by both countries were only part of their aircraft carrier building plans for the 1920s and 1930s and were not, by themselves, arms races but, when combined with the increased conventional fleet carriers built by the United States in the 1930s and the growing feeling that aircraft carriers might be the battleships of World War II, suggested an arms race that was the most important part of the naval war in the Pacific. Many people in the United States and the United Kingdom were not convinced of the supremacy of aircraft carriers until after Pearl Harbor; by 1942 there was a consensus that there was a critical arms race between the United States and Japan for the most large-sized aircraft carrier decks in the Pacific Ocean. While Japan would have been beaten in that race by the United States regardless of what happened during 1942 in the Pacific, the Battle of Midway really decided the matter early on when the Japanese navy lost four carriers in the course of a few hours in June of 1942 to one lost in the battle by the United States. The ability of Japan to replace the lost carriers as well as to add to their fleet was but a small fraction of what the United States could produce in the same period. At the same time the quality of the previously superb Japanese aircrew members declined greatly as well.

Lexington was sunk in the Battle of the Coral Sea in 1942 as was a small Japanese carrier. Both *Akagi* and *Kaga* were sunk in the Battle of Midway a month later. The loss of the two Japanese battle cruiser conversions plus two other fleet carriers in one day balanced against the American loss of one fleet carrier, USS *Yorktown*, had a dramatic impact on the naval activities of both countries for the remainder of the war as well as demonstrating to the Japanese the vulnerability of their aircraft carriers whatever their ancestry. The final battle cruiser conversion, *Saratoga*, survived the war.

By the early 1930s it was becoming clear that the Great War might not have been the War to End All Wars. Germany was beginning to look like a big problem again in spite of the loss of weapons, industry, territory and allies from her status in 1918. The appointment of Adolph Hitler as the Chancellor of Germany in 1933 was, or at least in hindsight should have been, a call to arms for France, Poland, Denmark, the

Netherlands and Belgium. France actually anticipated some aspects of the situation and the decline in the chances of continuing peace. It had probably contributed to that decline by leaving the German Rhineland (the industrial heartland of Germany which France had occupied since the end of World War I) in 1930. The Rhineland was supposed to have been demilitarized after 1929 when the French announced that its troops would leave but that objective was never met. Finally, in 1936 Germany sent its troops into the Rhineland to return it fully to German control. Many felt at the time that this action would bring on war between Germany and France which would have been disastrous for Germany since its army at that time consisted of only about 18,000 combat troops. The French army was far larger and by calling up the reserves it could have put over a million troops into the Rhineland in short order. The French complained about the German occupation but did not act. The situation had in fact begun to deteriorate three years previously when Hitler had seized power in Germany. Many of Hitler's military decisions during World War II generated amusement and relief among his enemies and dismay among his generals but his decisions, both political and military, during the mid to late thirties were generally brilliant notwithstanding the serious reservations about them by most of his advisers.

Hitler's rise to power was a spur to both Britain and France to look to their military establishments. Neither was very happy with what it saw. The French had begun their Maginot Line in 1929 as a defense against possible attacks from Germany. The point of the Line was not as permanent protection for France but rather was intended to delay potential German aggression from the east until the French army had time enough to be assembled and positioned. Where it was built, the Line was a well thought out but static defense on France's border with Germany. Unfortunately for France it did not cover areas where the French thought that the topography would be impossible for the Germans to penetrate and areas where its borders were with neutral countries like Luxemburg, Belgium and Switzerland. The French were wrong with regard to the Germans respecting neutral nations except for their avoidance of attacking Switzerland as to which there may have been other factors involved. The French were also wrong about the Germans being deterred by very rough terrain.

The concerns of the French about German rearming gave them reason to look to other aspects of their defenses, especially after the rise of Hitler, and they, together with Great Britain, took stock of their conventional forces. At that stage Germany was not building much in the way of large surface ships for its navy. The two large battleships and the three pocket battleships (*Panzerschiffen*)[41] that Germany was to produce for World War II were not yet under way and the two predreadnought battleships left to Germany by the Versailles Treaty were museum pieces. Therefore neither Britain nor France had any incentive to build more or better battleships and thus neither an arms race nor an armament race appeared in this area. Note that the pocket battleships were begun in the midthirties and were on hand and fully operational at the beginning of World War II. The large battleships came on a little later but all the heavy ships were conceived and constructed in the usual four to five year period.

The land forces of the two countries were quite similar. Before the usual response "what about the German panzers" it must be noted that, notwithstanding the panzer blitzkrieg at the beginning of the war, at that time the French had more tanks than the Germans and their tanks were bigger with more powerful armament. Thus there was not much of an armament race and the arms race, such as it was, was won by France. But in the German invasion of France the war was won by the German armor by virtue of its tactics, winning the battles which involved tanks not because their tanks more numerous overall but because they were more concentrated at the points of the German attacks. It was tactics, not the numbers or the quality of the tanks, that powered the blitzkrieg and defeated France. The German tactics worked because the French

---

41   *Panzerschiffen* (armored ships) was the German title for the ships of this class. Pocket battleship was the British name for the ships in the class. Given the 11 inch guns in the ships' main batteries, the British name seems more appropriate. There was a potential for an armament race here but no country besides Germany participated and the German pocket battleships did not have glorious careers.

were devoted to their concept of armor as an adjunct to infantry and artillery and not, as the Germans did, using their tanks as a separate force. Never fully answered was the obvious question. If the Germans had massed their somewhat outnumbered and outgunned tanks at critical points to make their breakthroughs, why did the French not use their tanks to attack the Germans in the areas from which the German had stripped their panzers? This is quite similar to the situation existing in the discussion of envelopments in which the army attempting an envelopment had to mask the weakening of its forces in contact with the enemy as a result of its diversion of the enveloping troops. The likely reason that the French did not exploit that weakness is probably some combination of a basic defense-oriented French military strategy and because the French had very little intelligence about forces and activity behind the German lines. This produced great uncertainty about the locations of German forces other than those with which the French were in contact at the time.

World War II

In any case there were no armament races between the French and Germans with respect to tanks and the tank arms race was close. If there were a winner in this respect it should have been the French. The German victory was the product of better tactics and perhaps better soldiers. There were, however, at least three major armament races in connection with World War II. In the order of their initiation they were radar, the atomic bomb and the B-29 (Superfortress) heavy bomber.

It is at least necessary to mention what seems to have been an unusual absence of an armament race. All but one of the major participants in World War II used, as their most common weapon early in that war, rifles which were very similar to, and sometimes the same as, the bolt-action rifles they had used over two decades earlier in World War I. The exception was the United States which, except for sharpshooters and snipers for whom it retained the conventional bolt action Springfield rifle from the early 1900s, used a newly designed semiautomatic rifle, the Garand or M-1.[42] This rifle enabled the shooter to fire all of the rounds in its magazine simply by pulling the trigger for each round. With more conventional rifles the shooter, after firing a shot, had to open the bolt, draw it back and discharge the cartridge case of the previous shot, push the bolt forward picking up the next cartridge from the magazine and seating it in the chamber and finally locking the bolt in the firing position. In the course of this procedure the hammer would be cocked. The shooter then had to aim the weapon and pull the trigger. While the working of the bolt action would take only a few seconds, in combat that might seem to be an eternity. Nevertheless,

---

42   There is sometimes confusion between the M-1 rifle and the M-1 carbine. The carbine was a smaller and lighter weapon intended for a soldier whose principal duty was not as a rifleman. It also was a .30 caliber semiautomatic weapon but it fired a much less powerful round than the M-1 rifle. The M-2 carbine was similar to the M-1 carbine except that it could be fired fully automatically as well as semiautomatically.

the bolt-action rifles were a huge improvement over the American Civil War weapons. The commands for loading and firing such weapons told a great deal. They were, for each shot, load, handle cartridge, tear cartridge, charge cartridge, draw rammer, ram cartridge, return rammer, prime, aim, fire and recover arms.[43]

It was not at all that the other participants in World War II were unable to produce a semiautomatic rifle. Most of them even equipped some of their forces with semi-automatic pistols. But many felt that there were legitimate reasons not to provide infantrymen with semiautomatic weapons. First, because of the complicated mechanism semi-automatic weapons were generally more prone to problems. Second, there was a general feeling that such weapons were less accurate. Third, there was a presumed logistical problem in that semiautomatic weapons would create a shortage of ammunition because the rate of fire would be so high.[44] Offsetting these negative factors, in addition to the high rate of fire available from semiautomatic weapons was the fact that it is easier to hold the sights of a semiautomatic rifle on a target since one does not have to operate the bolt. It should be noted in this context that during World War II most armies equipped some of their infantry units with short ranged, often large caliber, semiautomatic or fully automatic weapons. Nevertheless, no other country competed with the United States with respect to semiautomatic rifles. This avoidance of an armament race in rifles was only because the other major powers in World War II which could have developed semiautomatic or even fully automatic rifles simply chose not to do so at least early in the war. The technology was well known and was used in one form or the other by all of the small arms producing countries in their hand guns and submachine guns.

---

43 See Commands for Loading and Firing a Musket, from *Hardee's Rifle and Infantry Tactics* (1856) in Ayres, *A Military Miscellany* (2006).

44 This argument has been used against every improvement in the ability to fire small arms and automatic weapons more rapidly, including the concept of cartridges rather than powder, bullet and wadding loading. Speed prevailed over logistical difficulties, eventually, in all cases.

Returning to the actual major armament races of importance in World War II, radar (RAdio Detecting And Ranging) is essentially a radio that sends out a directional radio signal and receives that signal back if it strikes something which will reflect radio waves. The phenomenon had been noticed by some early experimenters with radio, notably by David Sarnoff of Radio Corporation of America when radio messages he was sending from his office in Manhattan to his laboratory in New Jersey were sometimes interrupted and reflected back by large ships in the Hudson River. By the mid-nineteen thirties both the United States and Great Britain had created radar sets, with the Germans and the Italians not far behind. Again we see a four to six year period of conception. development and combat readiness. Great Britain put its development into use quickly and built two lines of radar stations along the southeast coast of England. These of course were very important in the latter part of 1940 when the *Luftwaffe* was attacking England in force. Radar thus showed its importance early on in the war. The early British sets were not very precise because, among other things, they operated on a relatively low radio frequency which, although operating with longer range signals, did not enable the system to define its targets very well. All of the participants in the war were trying to develop small ideal radar sets with long range and precision target resolution but without much success until the British came up with a very remarkable solution. It was called the cavity magnetron. This seemingly simple device made the radar of British and American planes and ships far superior to that of their enemies, winning the very important armament race for detecting, identifying and destroying enemy forces. There are those who feel that it was more important even than that.[45]

The second major development that won an armament race in World War II was the United States invention of the atomic bomb. As it turned out, there was only one other competitor in the race. The United States government began to consider an atomic bomb after Albert Einstein wrote to President Roosevelt in 1939 describing his

---

45 See, for example, Buderi, *The Invention That Changed the World* (1997), *passim*.

thought that it might be possible to build a very powerful bomb using unstable atoms.[46] The President and his advisers thought that this idea should be thoroughly considered and, if it seemed feasible, should be undertaken. If the preliminary estimates of the potential power generated by such an explosion were correct, an atomic bomb could end the war. It seemed to some atomic physics researchers that the effort had enough of a chance of success to justify the expense which turned out to be in the neighborhood of $2,000,000,000. While the United States obviously won the atomic bomb armament race, as it turned out it was not much of a race. The British had the talent and the productive capacity to have engaged in the race for the bomb. They figured, quite correctly, that the United States had both more human resources and more money to do the job if indeed it could be done and they had nothing to fear from the Americans. Germany too had the ability to make a try to develop the bomb. If it had succeeded first the world would be a very different place today. Germany was greatly handicapped by the loss of top notch scientific minds in the thirties when the rise of Nazi anti-Semitism drove much of the talent necessary for the task out of the country. Germany effectively dropped out of the competition fairly early on. The Soviet Union knew a great deal about the atom bomb work being done in the United States thanks to its American and British spy networks but decided to wait for World War II to end before determining whether it was worth the huge diversion of resources to try to build such a bomb. As is well known the United States effort was successful and initially produced enough fissionable material by mid-1945 for three bombs. The first bomb was a test explosion in New Mexico which, notwithstanding some serious doubts even by its creators, was a success. The second and third bombs were dropped from the only aircraft that could have carried those bombs from the Mariana Islands to the target cities in Japan, the B-29. The second and third bombs also were successful and, between the damage done by those bombs and the United States threat to go ahead and

---

46 The letter although signed by Einstein was written by Leo Szilard based on his work in Germany before he escaped to London in 1933. He felt that Einstein's name as the author would carry more weight with President Roosevelt. Szilard later came to the United States.

destroy every city in Japan with atomic bombs, Japan decided to end the war. Again the period from conception to a useful weapon was five or six years.

The third major World War II development that won an armament race was the B-29 bomber. It was a major development not so much because it dropped the atomic bombs on Hiroshima and Nagasaki as because of its ability to bomb Japan generally. The B-29 had been dropping conventional incendiary and general purpose bombs on Japan for many months before it delivered the two atomic bombs. After teething problems and the movement of the B-29s operations from China to the Mariana Islands, the bombers made some very effective incendiary raids on Japanese cities. One of those raids, on Tokyo in March of 1945, killed and injured more people than either of the atomic bomb raids on Hiroshima and Nagasaki and burned out huge sections of Tokyo. Obviously the armament race was won by the United States, in large measure because the possible conventional competition for the B-29 was the German "New York" or "Amerika" bomber which was abandoned before it got very far along, leaving the very long range bomber field to the B-29.[47] Had the Germans succeeded with their extremely long-range bomber it would have been more a propaganda tool than a military weapon since the bomb load would have needed to be minuscule given the fuel necessary to travel from Europe to the United States and return. Even without competition the B-29 was almost not completed. It was far too great a change in technology to cover easily in one jump but the decision was made to try. Without an aircraft with the range of the B-29 the bombing of Japan with conventional and atomic bombs would have been much delayed and other islands controlled by the Japanese would have to have been

---

47   The Japanese had a plan to bomb the United States with large four engine flying boats (Kawanashi H8K (Emilys)) being refueled on route by specially equipped Japanese submarines. The raids never happened although if they had been carried out, the damage to the United States would have been mainly psychological. The flying boats could only carry about a ton of bombs and were quite slow so, in addition to being unable to do much harm, their survival was quite unlikely. Horn, *The Second Attack on Pearl Harbor* (2005), *passim*.

captured at terrible cost in both casualties and equipment. On the other hand, in order for the B-29 to function as it was contemplated a number of original concepts had to work. The aircraft was the first strategic bomber to be pressurized. All previous bombers had the air pressure within their fuselages at the same level as that of the ambient air. This required the crews to wear oxygen masks at least above 10,000 feet and often lower. Oxygen masks are cumbersome, not always effective and unpleasant to use, particularly above a pressure altitude of about 30,000 feet when the oxygen has to be pumped into the wearer's lungs under pressure and the wearer is forced to blow the oxygen out. This was very uncomfortable, tiring and made talking on the radio and intercom extremely awkward. Thus a pressurized fuselage was a great advantage to the crew without even considering the fact that it also allowed the aircraft to be heated although this is rarely mentioned. On the other hand some pictures of the crews at work show them working in much less clothing than would be necessary at altitude if the aircraft were at the ambient temperature. This was an enormous advantage at an altitude where the ambient temperature could well be 20 or 30 degrees below zero Fahrenheit. But pressurizing and heating the aircraft was difficult. The crew in each B-29 was divided into three groups each with its own controlled environment to limit the amount of area inside the fuselage that had to be controlled. The bulk of the crew was stationed in the forward "bubble," the three gunners who controlled their guns by remote control were in the center "bubble" and the tail gunner was in his own lonely "bubble."

These three armament races will be discussed further because they had an extraordinary impact on World War II.

It is often said that an aircraft which looks good performs well and vice versa. In general there may be something in this but exceptions abound. The A-5 (originally the A3J) (Vigilante) was an extremely handsome Navy aircraft that never really worked as well as projected in service. The F-102 (Delta Dagger) looked as though it was traveling at its projected top speed of Mach 1.2 while sitting on the ramp; it never went faster than about Mach 0.8 in the air.[48] The B-29 also fell into the exception mode. It looked very good with its narrow wings, streamlined fuselage and recessed gun turrets but it had a host of development problems.[49] The most serious were with the four new R-3350 Wright radial engines. The United States had been most fortunate in its supply of aircraft engines for use in World War II. Both Pratt & Whitney and Wright had developed very good radial engines of almost identical size in the mid-1930s, the P&W R-1820 and the W R-1830, the numbers referring to the cubic inch capacity of the cylinders in the engines. Although cubic capacity does not equate to horsepower, those numbers tended to indicate roughly the relative horsepower generated by those engines. Those engines powered most of the radial engine powered aircraft used early in the war. The next pair of radial engines was made up of the W R-2600 and the P&W R-2800. These engines powered many of the aircraft developed later in the war. Many would say that the P&W R-2800 was the best radial engine ever built.[50] Neither of these later engines generated enough power for the B-29 so a new and even larger engine was needed. Wright was chosen to build the new engine, the W R-3350. While the later larger World War II engines produced about 50% more power than either of the pair of the earlier series of radial engines, the W R-3350 increased the available power by only about 25% over its predessors. It would seem that this would be an easier increase in power than the previous one but it was not so. Walter Boyne suggests that six years would have been a reasonable time

---

48   The F-102 should not be confused with the F-102A which was the F-102 with its fuselage destreamlined in accordance with the just-discovered aerodynamic "area rule." The F-102A did not look as attractive as the F-102 but it flew as fast as had been projected for the F-102.

49   It may have been an example of Murphy's Law but the B-29 was one of the few American aircraft of that era which did not have an alternative aircraft in case the B-29 did not perform as planned. It was one that needed it.

50   Radial engines were favored for most aviation purposes by the United States military. They had more frontal area than inline engines so they created more drag but since they were air cooled they were not disabled by damage to the liquid cooling system of the more streamlined inline engines. Radial engines were often difficult to start but once running they could take a considerable amount of battle damage and continue to operate.

to design, build, test and adjust a completely new engine.[51] Wright had only three years to develop and test the W R-3350. There were many engine failures of the W R-3350s in military service[52] but after the war the civilian version of the engine powered the last of the large propeller-driven airliners quite successfully. It may have been that the full six years of testing and improvements had by then passed which made the difference although it seems more likely that the military engines, at least as used in the B-29s, were run much harder than the later civilian ones. Again the time from the first contract to combat use was four years and to the atomic bombings of Japan was five years

Not generally appreciated was the work of some B-29s against the Japanese merchant fleet. Their work was greatly overshadowed by the B-29s incendiary attacks on Japanese cities and by the atomic bombings, but some B-29s were also used to mine the waters around the Home Islands of Japan. Those mines did severe damage. In late 1944 and the first half of 1945 more Japanese merchant ships were sunk by those mines than were sunk by American submarines during the whole war. The comparison is misleading. By late in the war Japan had run short of large merchant ships and, out of desperation, was using many smaller ships which were the ones usually sunk by mines. This usually much misunderstood aspect of the Pacific War will be discussed further on.

It would probably be appropriate to mention briefly a bizarre Japanese plan to bomb the United States toward the end of the war although the plan hardly qualified as a participant in an armament race

---

51 Boyne, *Clash of Wings* (1994), p. 360. This is probably not a bad rule of thumb for aircraft of that era as well. Unfortunately that much time was not often available for aircraft either.

52 The worst B-29 engine problem known to the author in which the crew survived happened to a member of his all-weather fighter squadron. He had been the pilot of a B-29 which had lost one of its engines shortly after takeoff. He declared an emergency and came back into the traffic pattern where he lost a second engine. As he was on final approach to landing he lost a third engine and landed on one engine which had been so overstressed by then that it was not repairable. He transferred out of B-29s and into fighters.

with the United States and Japan trying to develop ways to do strategic bombing to each other's territory. The Japanese response, developed over a shorter period than the three to six year development period, to the American effort to build and put into use a way of bombing the Japanese from B-29s was to launch a barrage of thousands of hydrogen-filled paper balloons with small incendiary bombs attached. This sounds a lot like a scene from a comic opera but it was more than that. Most of the balloons were indeed made of paper but it was a particular form of paper that contained the hydrogen very well. In addition the balloons were equipped with a barometric device to release some of the hydrogen if the balloon rose above the level of the jet stream and to release some of the ballast if the balloon dropped below the level of the jet stream. The hope was that at least a few of them would ride the very strong east-flowing jet stream over Japan to the American northwest where the bombs would start forest fires. Some did so and produced six deaths and some small forest fires. The fact that fewer than 10% (the actual number is quite uncertain) of the bombs reached the United States and appeared in a large number of states (including a few which landed as far east as the Midwest) was somewhat surprising as was the fact that the Japanese launched the balloons in the fall and winter of 1944-45 when the targeted forests of the American northwest were damp and hard to ignite.

The B-29 was an excellent example of the problems facing a military service venturing into uncharted areas of new equipment which might become involved in an armament race. There were very serious risks. For the B-29 to perform the mission for which it was intended it had to carry a large bomb load rapidly for long distances and deliver it accurately. All aircraft, like other types of complicated machinery, contain a series of compromises. Subsonic aircraft speed is largely a function of engine power and lifting ability. Aircraft wings are, among other things, a compromise between lift and drag; in general a thin wing is likely to create less drag and therefore allow the aircraft to travel faster but again in general a thin wing will have less lifting capacity. One good way to minimize those types of risks if one has the assets and the time to do so is to have several similar products in the pipeline simultaneously. Then even if serious problems develop in one the others might still be viable. The United States was extremely fortunate to have had the time, the talent and the assets to do this with aircraft before and during World War II and to have had, early in the war, good luck with the results. For land-based pursuit aircraft the Army Air Force, at the beginning of the United States participation in World War II, had the more than acceptable P-38 (Lightning), the P-39 (Airacobra)[53] and the P-40 (Tomahawk) and during the last two years of the war had the superb P-47 (Thunderbolt) and P-51 (Mustang). For medium bombers both the B-25 (Mitchell) at the beginning of the war and the B-26 (Marauder) a little later were operational. The B-25 served throughout the war and the B-26, after some initial problems were solved, served well in the latter part of the war. For heavy bombers the B-17 (Flying Fortress) was available at the beginning of the war and the B-24 (Liberator) shortly after that.

The United States Navy did something similar. For fighters early in the war there were the F4F (Wildcat) and the F2A (Buffalo).[54] By later in the war the Navy had replaced the unsatisfactory torpedo bomber, the TBD (Devastator) with the very successful TBF (Avenger) and the slow but effective SBD (Dauntless) dive bomber was replaced not so successfully by the SB2C (Helldiver).[55] For most of the war the F6F (Hellcat) and the F4U (Corsair) handled the brunt of the Pacific fighter action. They were helped greatly by the failure of the Japanese to improve significantly on the carrier fighters with which they started the

---

53   Although almost 10,000 planes were built. the P-39 was not as well known as the P-38 and the P-40. In large measure this was due to the fact that approximately one-half of the P-39 production was given to the Soviet Union which used them as ground attack aircraft because of their 37mm cannon. Additionally the P-39 suffered from poor high altitude performance due to the absence of superchargers which were in short supply in the United States.

54   The F2A was often belittled and seldom used by the Navy, but the F2As sold to Finland had an extraordinary combat record. See Greer, *World in Conflict* (2004), pp. 60-61.

55   The very informal names that the air and ground crews derived from the designators of their dive bombers said it all. The SBD was called "Slow But Deadly" and the SB2C was called "Son of a Bitch, Second Class."

war and the Japanese inability to maintain their extremely high prewar pilot standards which were reached in a very difficult flight program designed to produce only about 100 graduate pilots a year. These United States Navy aircraft all made very significant contributions to the American war effort.

The B-29 was such a massive effort, with an end cost of a staggering $3,000,000,000, that a parallel aircraft design was not attempted for very long during the B-29 five year development period. The wisdom of an attempt at a parallel program was evident in the B-29 situation. Of course there was no assurance that an alternative design would have served any better given the many innovations required for the aircraft but it might have worked. We shall never know.

The three armament races are examples of three different types of armament races. The radar race was the most conventional. The winner with the best radar would have the best control over the battlefield, whether in the air, on land or on the sea and would have the best chance of prevailing. "Best" in this case could mean longer range, better target definition, more reliability, smaller size or lighter weight or perhaps even more convenience of use. Range tended to be governed largely by the power of the radar which in turn required a better system to generate signals on the best radar frequencies for the intended use and an antenna system well located for the task. Range was particularly important for early warning radar. Fire control radar for aiming guns, cannons, rockets or bombs did not require high power as much as much as good definition of the target. This in turn required much higher radar frequencies which initially were very difficult to generate, especially at high power.[56] Ground mapping radar and navigational radar were rather a mixture of both. The concept of radar was known before World War II and early warning radar had been deployed

---

56 The British invented the cavity magnetron which produced powerful very high frequency signals and guaranteed to the United States and the United Kingdom an enormous radar advantage over their enemies for several years until the Germans obtained a cavity magnetron from a crashed Royal Air Force bomber the self-destruction device on which did not function.

and became operational on parts of the southeast coast of England just before World War II began. It operated on what were, by radar standards, very low frequencies. The lower the frequency the larger the necessary antenna, the longer the usable range and the easier to generate the signal. The higher the frequency the smaller the antenna, the shorter the range, the better the target definition and the more difficult it was to generate the signal. Thanks to the retrieval of a cavity magnetron from the British bomber the Germans gained the ability to build better radar sets capable of operating on a number of higher radar bands but only for the last year or so of the war. In spite of occasional exchanges of technical data between Germany and Japan, the Japanese did not seem to be able to operate on the higher radar frequencies. Accordingly the Japanese radar was not able to operate efficiently on many frequencies which would have been useful for different purposes. It is impossible to quantify the advantage enjoyed by Great Britain and the United States through their use of radar during World War II but the advantage certainly was huge.

The atomic bomb armament race with Germany did not turn out to be much of a race as the Germans effectively dropped out part way through it. Of course the United States did not know the state of Germany's efforts to make a bomb but the main purpose of the United States effort to build an atomic bomb was to use it against Japan in the hope that it would make an invasion unnecessary, reducing greatly the casualties. In fact the United States had been well ahead of the German efforts throughout the period when the German program was still working. The German-American race to build the atomic bomb resulted in a very unusual event. While the United States and Great Britain had been bombing the industrial centers of Germany to try to cripple its war effort, a fortuitous opportunity to delay the German atomic effort presented itself. A strange and rare molecule called heavy water was very useful in atomic research for slowing and/or blocking the emission of particles from radioactive materials, like Uranium 235 for example. Heavy water is a naturally occurring molecule. It looks like water and for most purposes behaves like water but instead of being composed of two hydrogen atoms and one oxygen atom, molecules of heavy water are made up of two atoms of deuterium and one atom of oxygen. Deuterium is an isotope of hydrogen which contains a proton and a neutron (rather than just a proton as is the case with ordinary water) in its nucleus. While heavy water is extremely rare, water in Norway has a somewhat higher content of heavy water than usual and the Germans, with great difficulty, had produced a supply of heavy water there. The Allies knew about the supply and attempted to bomb it. Those efforts were not effective except to the extent of convincing the Germans that their supply of heavy water would be safer in Germany. It became known that the supply was to be shipped on a ferry trip across a lake. The Norwegian underground arranged a timed explosion to sink the ferry in the middle of a lake in Norway. The explosion did exactly that although it also caused the death of some innocent Norwegian civilians who happened to be on board the ferry. The loss of the German supply of heavy water was a serious blow to the German atomic program and, together with other events, caused the program to be shut down before it was close to enabling the Germans to try to build a bomb. The race to build the "ultimate weapon" was in effect conceded to the Americans quite early in the process although it was by no means clear until much later that the American bombs would actually work. Of course in the event the Americans successfully completed the race which both ended the war and produced a very frightening postwar world.

The third armament race, the designing, building and deploying an aircraft to bomb Japan from great distances away, had no opposite enemy program to beat. By late in the war the Japan was not trying to bomb the United States or anywhere else at least in a strategic sense.[57] Its bombing by this time was purely tactical.[58] The armament race was

---

57 There were, in the course of the war, several Japanese plans to bomb the United States. One was the previously mentioned and relatively well known scheme to launch paper balloons carrying small incendiary bombs to the United States; see p. 63-64. Another largely unknown plan was to use large flying boats refueled by submarines in protected anchorages to bomb the West Coast of the United States and the Panama Canal. See generally Horn, *The Second Attack on Pearl Harbor* (2005).

58 Most of this tactical bombing was of a new and particularly effective type –

a race against the clock. The B-29 was needed to deliver the atomic bombs as soon as the bombs were ready and the B-29s could be used in the interim, if there were a gap, to test the aircraft in actual strategic bombing operations over Japan to try to avoid having any sort of problem when an atomic bomb was aboard. This was also rather a fallback use of the B-29 if the plane was successful but the bomb was not. It was well that there was adequate time available at least to test the B-29 more before the atomic bomb flights. Even with that testing the B-29 was not a reliable aircraft. For example, on the day before the first atomic bomber was dispatched there were four crashes on the takeoffs of B-29s from Tinian.[59] If the B-29 had proved a failure there was no comparable bomber in the development pipeline until the much later B-36 (Peacemaker) or B-50 (also Superfortress).[60] That would have meant more island landings by marines and army forces and far more work by Navy construction battalions to try to create air bases in the Bonin and Ryukyu Islands, a distance of roughly 650 nautical miles from Tokyo, with long enough runways to enable B-17s and B-24s to bomb most of the Japanese Home Islands.

As it turned out, the armament race against time to build the B-29 and put it into squadron service in spite of its serious problems was won, more or less. The B-29 was first used for conventional bombing of Japan from bases in China but the results were not satisfactory. The bombs were not hitting their targets. Most of that problem was not with the B-29s or their crews but was caused by bombing from high altitudes which was entirely consistent with the planning which went into the B-29. The winds over Japan were often of jet stream speeds. It was only after the Mariana Islands were secured and air bases built on

---

suicide bombing by flying bomb-carrying aircraft into targets, mainly naval ships involved in landing operations on Japanese-held islands. See Morison, *United States Naval Operations in World War II*, vol. XIV (1968), pp. 52 *et seq.*

59 It was for this reason that a decision was made on the day before the mission to arm the atomic bomb in the air after takeoff rather than on the ground before takeoff so as not to wipe out the island if the plane crashed.

60 The B-50 was essentially a B-29 with the much more powerful P&W R-4360 engines.

them that the B-29s could bomb Japan with any degree of regularity and effectiveness for the half year before the atomic bombs were ready to be dropped in early August of 1945. The 20th Air Force, which controlled the B-29s, eventually concluded that the high altitude conventional bombing for which the B-29 had been designed would not work in many circumstances in Japan because of the very high winds through which the bombs released from high altitudes had to drop. These winds not only moved the bomb patterns in unpredictable directions, they also spread the bomb pattern out. Both of these factors greatly affected adversely the incendiary bombing accuracy and effect. Medium altitude bombing was then tried very successfully, partially because the lower altitude as a simple matter of geometry reduced the errors in the system but principally because the bombing then took place entirely below the jet stream. The form of construction of Japanese cities made incendiary bombing extremely effective particularly when the proper spacing of those bombs was worked out so as to create large fires on the ground. This was shown best in the raid on Tokyo in March of 1945 which created a fire storm that burned out large areas of the center of the city, killing more people than either of the atom bombs. One might well ask why the United States did not continue with the burning out of Japanese cities either for humanitarian reasons because we were quite uncertain about what amount of damage the atom bomb would cause or to conceal the existence of United States atomic bombs from the world. The answer seems to be that the policy makers in the United States felt that the Japanese would not surrender just because their cities were being burned out. Something additional was thought to be necessary and that thought turned out to be a two-pronged approach.

The first prong was the obvious one. Drop two atomic bombs on major Japanese cities doing terrible damage and providing great object lessons. The second prong was to notify the Japanese after the second bomb that the United States would continue to destroy Japan one city at a time until it surrendered. The second prong was pure bluff. There were no more atomic bombs then available nor would there be another one until either in November of 1945 by some estimates or as late as sometime in January of 1946 by others. The limiting factor on the production of more bombs was the very slow process of extracting enough fissionable isotopes from uranium or plutonium to permit the manufacture of the additional bombs. The Japanese, or at least their emperor, were fooled by the bluff, perhaps helped a bit in that direction by the entry of the Soviet Union into the war against Japan at the time of the second bomb. While the surrender decision was based almost entirely on the American bluff, the emperor made a decision for his country that was about the best course he could have taken. Had he not surrendered, the firebombing would have continued and the Japanese would have lost at least large parts of a number of their cities before the American invasion of the Home Islands began on November 1, 1945. If that invasion still had to be made, it was generally conceded by American planners that American and allied casualties would probably have been on the order of the American casualties for the whole rest of the war, or about 400,000 killed. Given the Japanese plans for the defense of the Home Islands involving, among other things, civilians armed with sharpened sticks participating in the defense, one could safely assume that the Japanese fatalities would have been well into the millions. Ironic as it seems, the United States might well have done the Japanese a great favor by dropping the atomic bombs. Although the deaths and residual radiation from the bombs were very serious, those deaths and effects were far less than those which would have occurred as the result of an invasion and conquest of the Home Islands, to say nothing about the losses from fire bombings of Japanese cities in the meantime. Additionally, the American occupation of the Home Islands after such an invasion would almost certainly have been far harsher on the Japanese than was actually the case.

World War II, in spite of its almost six-year span, had relatively few armament races initiated during the war. There were many very serious arms races but production seemed to be more important than innovation in the early 1940s. There were a few notable exceptions beyond those previously discussed that are often considered to have been products of the war years. Perhaps among the most important were the German V weapons, the V-1 and the V-2. These were unmanned missiles fired from Europe into England. The V-1 was an air breathing, winged missile with a large warhead that flew relatively low from France or the Low Countries into southeast England and was generally aimed at London although its guidance system was not very precise. It traveled at about the speed of fighter aircraft and could therefore be shot down if defending fighters were vectored into the correct position in time. The V-2 was a ballistic missile also launched from Western Europe but it traveled at a very high altitude and was extremely fast so it could not be destroyed by aircraft or by any other means then available. The V-2s' guidance system was also imprecise, but for terror weapons random explosions are probably a more effective threat to the general populace than missiles dropping accurately around military objectives. The only way to destroy V-2s was to bomb them on their launching pads or earlier in their production or testing period. Neither the shooting down of the V-1s or efforts to destroy the launching sites of both missiles were very effective but, since the missile barrage had not begun until after the invasion of Europe in the summer of 1944, the Allied armies soon overran the missile launching areas. The V designation stood for "retaliation weapon," "reprisal weapon," or "vengeance weapon," being various translations of *vergeltungwaffe*. Since work was started on both missiles prior to the beginning of the war when there was probably no concept of necessary reprisals, the V names were substituted for the original names later in the war in an attempt to justify their use if indeed justification were needed at that stage of the war. In any case these arms projects started before the war and the Allies did not participate in the race so there was in this area not only no armament race during the war but no armament race at all. The Germans had the field entirely to themselves.

Jet aircraft are assumed by many to have been the subject of an armament race during the war but here too they predate the war by a fair amount. The jet engine for aircraft was patented by Frank Whittle, the patent having been applied for in Great Britain in 1930. By 1937 experimental jet engines were running on both sides of the Channel. The Heinkel 178 flew even before World War II began, the British Gloster first flew in 1941 as a test bed for a jet engine and the best jet aircraft of the war, the Me 262, first flew in 1942 and was flying operationally over Germany in 1944, giving Germany the first place in both the armament race and the arms race for jet fighters. In a sense this paralleled the World War I experience with the Fokker D.VII. In both cases the Germans won the races but the wars were lost. Even the United States which lagged badly in the jet race ordered some jet fighters before Pearl Harbor and made the first flight in the P-59A (Airacomet)[61] in 1942.

Notice what these numbers indicate. Whereas in World War I new planes could be created and put into service in a matter of months to respond to planes put into service by the enemy, by World War II the aircraft were so complex that designing, building and testing them took about as long in years as the previous war's aircraft took in months. In the early part of World War II there was, however, a rare exception. Shortly before the United States entered the war the British were trying to buy aircraft manufactured in the United States. North American Aviation, instead of building more of some existing United States pursuit aircraft, offered to build them an entirely new plane in 120 days.[62] It did so, producing the best propeller-driven fighter of the war, the P-51.

Notwithstanding this rare exception, it was usually felt that there was not much sense in starting a complicated project like a new aircraft for World War II as late as 1942, for the general view was that the war would be over one way or the other by 1945, well before any new complicated project could be completed, put out into the field and used operationally. There was, of course, one seemingly very large exception in World War II, that of the atomic bomb. Even that, however, was not really within the three-year horizon because there was not an actual completion of the project in 1945. The three bombs, including the

---

61   The Airacomet as a pursuit ship was no better than its name.

62   The aircraft was without an engine for the next several months because the Army Air Force had earmarked the supplies of the best American inline engine (the Allison V-1710) for its own use. In the long run the P-51 was powered largely by Rolls-Royce Merlin engines or by Packard-built Merlins and not many by the Allison engine with which it was originally equipped.

test bomb, that were exploded in 1945 were prototypes. They were not identical weapons. They even used different explosive material[63] and were very differently designed bombs.

World War II was, of course, full of arms races. Many times it was felt by some in hindsight that better, not more, weapons would have been a preferable course. One such area was in tank design. As was described earlier[64] the issue could sometimes be decided by neither numbers of men nor the quantity or quality of the equipment; it could be the result of better tactics. Sometimes it was such a combination of factors that it was impossible to credit any one factor. Sometimes there were arms races of a serious nature in which several combatants were producing a great deal of certain material which would not be used against the enemy's similar material, submarines for example.

Both before and during World War II there were arms races in several classes of naval vessels involving Japan, the United States, Germany and the United Kingdom. Germany had produced submarines which had constituted a serious menace to British trade routes in World War I and, not surprisingly, when rearming in the thirties modern submarines were high on Germany's priority list principally for the same purpose. While Germany's World War II submarines were much better than those of World War I they were generally not of a type unique enough that it would rate an armament race label. The Royal Navy responded to the German submarine building program not by increasing its submarine building as would have been done in a traditional arms race but rather by building a number of anti-submarine vessels, in large measure because submarines were not, until many years later, a good way to attack enemy submarines.

The Japanese and American navies increased their submarine fleets before and during World War II but neither did these fleets oppose each other. Their targets were their enemy's surface ships, both naval

---

63 Plutonium verses Uranium.

64 See pp.55-56

and merchant, although the Japanese concentrated largely on United States naval ships. While both countries used submarines for scouting, scouting by submarines was a much greater part of Japanese naval doctrine. Both of the "silent services" were active at in the early stages of the Pacific War. The American submarines were seriously affected by torpedo defects during the early stages of that war but thereafter did dreadful damage to the Japanese merchant marine. There was an interesting debate after the war between the United States Navy submarine force and the Army Air Force as to which service had done the most damage to the Japanese merchant marine during World War II. The submariners claimed a number of large merchant ships some of which could not be verified after the war and some of the tonnage estimates were reduced after the war when the facts became known.[65] The Air Force claimed many more ships sunk by the mines they dropped around the Home Islands toward the end of the war. As it turned out both services were correct. As the war progressed and the Japanese empire was shrinking dramatically, so did their supply of large cargo ships and tankers, mainly as a result of attacks by United States submarines. The smaller empire resulting had to be serviced by more of the surviving smaller ships in the Japanese merchant marine which, in the confined waters nearer Japan, were more vulnerable to air-dropped mines. In *The Oxford Guide to World War II* (Dear ed.), p. 495, there is a table (Table 6) that shows quite conclusively that in the earlier part of the Pacific War fewer but larger Japanese merchant ships were sunk but by the latter part of the war more but smaller ships were sunk. This seems to bear out both the Navy and Air Force claims.

Two ships of the class of the largest battleships in the world had been completed in Japan by early 1942 and the third was under construction.

---

65 On the other hand sometimes the tonnage estimates were corrected upwards. The worst case of underestimation was undoubtedly that of an aircraft carrier, HIJMS *Shanano*, which the United States Navy grudgingly allowed as a different 27,000 ton carrier. The ship sunk by the submarine USS *Archerfish* was in fact *Shanano*, a 70,000+ ton carrier (the biggest in the world by a large margin) of which the Navy was unaware. The Navy corrected the record after the war. See Enright, *Shanano!* (1987).

When the Battle of Midway was fought in June of 1942 resulting in the loss of four of the Japanese six fleet carriers, the Imperial Japanese Navy decided wisely that the third member of the class, HIJMS *Shanano*, should be converted to an aircraft carrier as had been done to battle cruisers under construction by both the Japanese and American navies after World War I. By late in 1944 she had been converted to a very large but quite inefficient aircraft carrier and replenishment ship. It really made no difference because she was sunk by a United States submarine after only one day at sea. The fourth member of the class was never built nor even named.

The six fleet carriers that had been built by the Japanese in the naval arms race between the wars were a fair match for the seven fleet carriers in which the United States Navy had built between the late twenties and the beginning of the Pacific War, particularly given the fact the United States had two oceans to protect with its carriers. There were some differences between the carrier designs of the two countries caused by the evolution of aircraft carrier designs of both countries as well as slightly different philosophies of the proposed purposes for which the carriers would be used. For example, the Japanese recognized the importance of launching all of the aircraft in a raid as close to the same time as possible since the flight endurance of a raid is limited. The flight endurance of the raid would be reduced to the time the first aircraft launched still had available when the whole raid had been launched. There might well have been an hour or more between the first and last planes launched in a full strike. In an attempt to be able to launch a strike faster the Japanese tried opening the bow of a carrier so they would be able to launch part of the carrier's air group from what would otherwise have been the forward part of the hanger deck. This idea was unsuccessful, in large measure because of the risk of the planes launching from the hanger deck colliding with planes launching from the flight deck above and because of the air turbulence generated by the hanger deck being closed at the rear. One might well also wonder about the ability of such a ship to deal with heavy seas while having a large opening in the bow.

In another desperate and ill-advised attempt to increase the carrier decks available, the Imperial Japanese Navy modified two elderly battleships by having their aft gun turrets and related equipment removed and replaced by short runways and other facilities related to aircraft. These hermaphrodite battleships were unsuccessful, at least as aircraft carriers, for a number of reasons not the least of which were that the aircraft had to take off what was effectively down wind from a short runway and could not land back on the battleship.

The Battle of Midway broke up the fleet carrier arms race and converted it into an arms rout. After Midway the Japanese were scrambling not only to replace the four fleet carriers which had been lost at Midway plus another smaller carrier lost at the Battle of the Coral Sea and a second smaller carrier lost later in the year in the Solomon Islands but also to try match the increased numbers of carriers which it knew the Americans were building. The Imperial Japanese Navy was spectacularly unsuccessful in this regard. While during the rest of the war after Midway the Japanese built 5 fleet carriers, 3 light carriers and several conversions of other non-navy vessels not all of which were able to see action,[66] the United States Navy built 17 fleet carriers, 9 light carriers and 77 escort carriers (small carriers built on merchant ship hulls).[67] In 1944 the United States was launching a carrier of one kind

---

66 Stille, *Imperial Japanese Navy Aircraft Carriers 1921-1945* (2005), p. 43. The classification of Japanese carriers other than fleet carriers is a little difficult. Some of which we might call light carriers were often labeled as escort carriers. The explanation of the confusion is that the United States built its light carriers on cruiser hulls and its escort carriers on merchant ship hulls so there was an easy delineation between the classes. The Japanese built both their light and escort carriers on merchant ship hulls not only because those hulls were more easily built although much weaker than navy hulls but also because the Japanese had built some merchant ships that could, in the event of war, be converted to carriers. They were. This both avoided the weight strictures of the naval treaties and masked the potential size of the Imperial Japanese Navy.

67 Morison, *History of United States Naval Operations in World War II*, vol. XV (1962), pp. 31-33. In addition to these carriers during the war, incredible as it seems United States shipyards had enough additional capacity to build 27 escort carriers for the Royal Navy under the Lend-Lease program.

or another each week. The carrier arms race turned into a debacle for the Japanese navy.

Landing craft was another category of military equipment as to which there was a very important arms race but the race was not against the enemy's similar equipment. It was rather against the clock. This was particularly important in the war against Germany. It had been obvious from the beginning of the war that if Germany were to be defeated Allied armies would have to be landed in Europe from the sea. The landing could have been into northwest Europe across the English Channel, into northern Europe at Norway or Denmark from the North Sea or in the south into Italy or the south of France from the Mediterranean Sea. There was a severe problem in constructing the thousands of vessels needed, from small landing craft to put a few troops on an enemy beach to very large ocean-going ships which could disgorge tanks directly onto a beach and everything in between. It was a further problem to have available enough of each category of vessels early on in order to provide training for the crews that would have to sail the landing craft into beaches under fire. These specialty vessels were so important to the landings in France that the invasion was postponed for a month to be able to have an extra month's production of landing craft available to the invading armies. Since the cross-Channel invasion was likely to be, in the language of Wellington about Waterloo, a near run thing, the Allies wanted as much assurance of victory as they could generate with overwhelming landing power.

While it turned out to be relatively unimportant in the long run, there was a bit of a naval arms race in another category. Until Pearl Harbor showed that aircraft could trump battleships, battleships had been the heart of modern navies. Navies were ranked in strength by the number of battleships they had. In the interim between World War I and World War II battleships went through significant changes. Shortly after the First World War the winners decided to limit the number of battleships each of the winners could have. The decisions required some countries to destroy modern ships, to convert them to other types of ships or to stop construction in mid-course. Germany, as a loser in

World War I, was entitled to keep only two ancient battleships and was prohibited from building new capital ships. The modern large ships in the German navy from World War I had been interned in Scapa Flow after the war and all were all lost when their crews scuttled them in 1919. When militarism resurfaced around 1930 Germany began to give thought to its navy. The submarine force was reestablished and light naval vessels were begun to be built, followed by a few cruisers and the so-called pocket battleships. Eventually the possibility of adding battleships and aircraft carriers to the new German navy was considered. While an aircraft carrier, *Graf Zeppelin*, was started but never finished, battleships were a form of naval status and the Germans thought that they needed them. On the other hand there was no way for Germany to compete with the number of ships in the combined battleship force of the British and American navies. The German solution was to try to build two battleships that were more powerful than any of the British and American battleships. So were born *Bismarck* and *Tirpitz* with greater displacement and heavier armor than the potentially competing battleships. Surprisingly the German ships did not have more powerful guns nor more of them than their presumed opponents so it is difficult for a realist to see why the Germans felt they could defeat the large numbers of American and British battleships. *Bismarck* made one war cruise on which she sank HMS *Hood,* an old but very large British battle cruiser, and damaged HMS *Prince of Wales,* a modern battleship just put into service, but *Bismarck* was in turn sunk by the Royal Navy. *Tirpitz* had a more ignominious demise, being bombed in Norwegian ports by the Royal Air Force without ever having dueled with another capital ship.

The Japanese did something similar. Although they were on the winning side in World War I, by the postwar naval treaties they were restricted to 60% of the ships possessed by the United States. Eventually this limitation so irked the Japanese that they withdrew from the naval treaties and started to build in 1937, in great secrecy hidden in large sheds, a class of four super battleships. Unlike the German so-called super battleships the Japanese ships really were super battleships with displacements almost twice those permitted by the naval treaties and with a main battery of 18 inch guns, also larger than permitted by the treaties. The first of this class, HIJMS *Yamato*, was completed in the fall of 1941 and participated as part of the covering force in the Pearl Harbor attack. She was sunk by United States Navy aircraft in 1945. The second, HIJMS *Musashi*, was completed shortly after the war began and served with the Japanese navy until the Battle for Leyte Gulf in 1944 when she was sunk by United States Navy aircraft. The third member of the class, HIJMS *Shanano*, the embarrassing fate of which has been previously discussed, lasted one day and the fourth was never built.

As a component of an arms race for battleships the German battleships seemed only to have performed the traditional function of a "fleet in being," the principal purpose of which was to force the enemy to commit maritime assets to watch those battleships in being in case they came into active service in the war at an inconvenient time. On the other hand, the Japanese super battleships fought together with the rest of the Japanese navy in conventional ways but their end result was similar to the German result. The Japanese battleships were also sunk but in this case without their sinking or damaging an enemy capital ship.

Postwar

After the end of World War II it might have been easy for the United States to have fallen into the same mode as it had after World War I. The size of its military declined sharply although the amount of leftover military hardware was huge. Aircraft, tanks and other vehicles plus large, gray-painted warships abounded. But on this occasion there were few illusions about a war to end all wars. While Germany and Japan were not likely to become military dangers for some time, if ever, the Soviet Union was gobbling up any Eastern European country that it could. It went as far west as its zone in partitioned Germany, as far southwest as Yugoslavia (at least presumed to be under the thumb of the Soviet Union) and as far south as Bulgaria and Rumania. While a few of the countries in the Soviet sphere were permitted to maintain some aura of independence, they were called, with good reason, Russian satellites. As the Soviet Union began to recover from the terrible effects of World War II on it and to become more outspokenly bellicose toward the West, concerns grew about a possible military confrontation between the Soviet Union and the West. Those concerns became more serious when, in 1948, the Soviet Union blockaded the road and rail access to the western zones of Berlin. The blockade was broken when the United States and the United Kingdom supplied Berlin by air throughout the winter of 1948-49. Just about the time when the Berlin blockade was broken, the Soviet Union went off in another and far more dangerous direction. It exploded its first atomic bomb. The result was that while the armament race for the atomic bomb had been won by the United States, the bomb was no longer a United States monopoly and an atomic bomb arms race began in earnest. Initially the atomic race was limited to bombs. In 1950 the Soviet Union's far-eastern satellite, North Korea, invaded South Korea. With this background the western democracies were compelled to keep their guard up. Particularly in that very rapidly changing sphere, air power, the requirements were changing rapidly. The United States and the United Kingdom were trying to match or exceed the Soviet Union's developments point by point. It was a true arms race with occasional developments that approached the level of armament races.

The arms race between the United States and the Soviet Union started at the end of World War II on a fairly even footing. The United States, although well behind Britain and Germany in the development of jet engines, had by then built two jet fighters (using British designed engines), the P-59A and the P-80 (Shooting Star). The former was a failure and the latter was quite successful for a straight wing aircraft at that time. The British also had some good jet fighters and, more importantly, made the best jet engines in the world. The Russians copied those engines, the Americans made them under license from Rolls-Royce. The United States was trying to keep up with the Russian aircraft development and was producing new fighter aircraft in the late 1940s and early 1950s at the rate of about one new model per year. The Russians were doing about the same. Between 1945 and 1955 the United States Air Force brought into service as fighters the P-80, the F-82 (Twin Mustang), the F-84 (Thunderjet), the F-86 (Sabre), the F-89 (Scorpion), the F-94, the F-100 (Super Sabre), the F-101 (Voodoo), the F-102A (Delta Dagger) and the F-104 (Starfighter).[68] This list does not take into account the large differences among several varieties of aircraft within a general category which made quite major changes in what should have been, based upon the model numbers, very similar aircraft. The F-84F, the F-86D, the F-86H, the F-89D, the F-89H, the F-89J, the F-94C, and the F-101B could well have been given separate numbers and for a short time some had different numbers. Probably for political purposes in the Congressional appropriation process, they did not keep the new numbers. The Soviet Air Force also went through a number of fighters during the same period but not as many as the United States Air Force. The United States Navy as well also went through a number of short-lived changes which were

---

68   Of course this does not mean that a plane was created from scratch to operational status each year. Several aircraft would be in various stages of development behind each new operational aircraft, keeping more or less to the 3 to 6 year development cycle..

quite comparable to the Air Force's experience. T. H. Thomason in his excellent book *U. S. Naval Air Superiority* says

"[I]t is interesting to compare and contrast the Navy's jet-fighter development record with that of the Air Force over the same period. Such a comparison is necessarily subjective but, roughly speaking, both services each contracted for about 24 jet fighter programs that reached flight status. Of those, five in each service were arguably failures, not meeting performance projections much less moving from development to operational status. Each service initiated one program that was clearly misconceived, the Navy's F2Y Sea Dart that was a supersonic jet fighter seaplane and the Air Force's diminutive F-85 parasite fighter that was to be launched and recovered from a bomber for self-protection. Three programs in the Navy – the F11F-1F, the F5D, and the F8U-8 did not proceed to production, not because they were not adequate in performance or handling qualities, but because another fighter was chosen instead. There were four similar programs in the Air Force, the F-87, F-91, F-93 and F-107. The remainder, 15 in the Navy and 15 in the Air Force, were used operationally and were produced in the hundreds, if not thousands, each."[69]

In bombers the United States in the same period built and put into service the B-45 (Tornado) (a jet bomber), the B-50 (basically a B-29 with more powerful engines), the B-36 (a very large bomber with six P&W R-4360 reciprocating engines and four jet engines), the B-47 (Stratojet, with six jet engines) and the B-52 (Stratofortress with eight jet engines). In the meantime the Russians had built their first production strategic bomber, the Tu-4 (a copy of a B-29 that had diverted to Siberia when it had been damaged over Japan). Premier

69 Thomason, *U. S. Naval Air Superiority* (2007), p. 264.

Stalin ordered a precise copy of the B-29 to be made for the Soviet Air Force over the objection of some senior officials of the Russian aviation industry who felt they could build a better bomber. The Tu-4 was not a success but a better jet strategic bomber, the Tu-16, followed. It was thought, at least by the United States Air Force, to be the rough equivalent of the American B-47 and if that were correct it would have been a difficult plane for the Americans to intercept with their radar net and their then available fighters.

It is important to keep in mind what the major function of fighter aircraft had been. It was, in large measure, to take on the enemy's fighters and defeat them. In the older terminology the fighters were to maintain at least air superiority over the territory that was assigned to them and preferably, in the age of atomic bombs, to achieve and maintain air supremacy in their assigned territory. To have any hope of achieving these goals the defensive fighter units would have to have received aircraft at least equal to those of their opponents' fighters and bombers and of course preferably superior.[70] If one's opponent was producing improved aircraft one had to try to stay ahead. This meant that many new aircraft had relatively short service life because they were outmoded quickly. Also contributing to the rapid turnover of fighters during the first half of the Cold War and the time when fighter defenses of the United States were critical were the changes in fighter armament during the period. These changes were more than simply increasing the size or number of cannons. During this period various types of rockets and later missiles became fighter armament, in time requiring fighters to be, to a larger degree than theretofore, built around their armament. In order to build speed and maneuverability into fighters, their weight had to be carefully controlled. This, in turn, limited the stress the fighters could take over long periods and contributed to their early retirement. By the second half of the Cold War fighters had become largely irrelevant when the principal weapons on both sides of

---

70 The fighter crews, at least those in the United States Air Force, knew that, even with excellent aircraft and ramming tactics, wiping out an attacking bombing force was almost impossible and any leakage at all of the bombers with nuclear weapons through the fighters and antiaircraft fire would be catastrophic.

the war were ballistic missiles since they were not able to be destroyed by fighters or any armament they could carry.

Other categories of important high speed Cold War aircraft on both sides of course had stresses and strength issues but not nearly to the degree that the fighters did. Additionally the bombers and transport aircraft were not in direct competition with each other so, while improved models were made by both sides, there was not the frantic rush to put rapidly built and tested aircraft of those types into service.

Consider what this rapid back-and-forth competition in aircraft design really meant. Both countries were conceiving, designing and building aircraft during supposed peace time at a rate that would, for the most part,[71] have been totally unacceptable even for the losing side in the midst of a war. The state of the art was changing so fast and the competition between the United States and the Soviet Union was so fierce that, at least on the American side, in spite of the three to six year development cycle aircraft became obsolescent very quickly. In addition, the sciences of aerodynamics and metallurgy, the new weapons which could be carried by those fighters and the airborne electronics that could be used by those fighters were all evolving very rapidly. New construction not only had to move very fast in dealing with the factors that were routine in aircraft but also new issues that started showing up as aircraft speeds increased. There were serious problems with the compressibility of air as the speeds increased toward the end of World War II. Aircraft began to approach the speed of sound in dives and became uncontrollable, often leading to crashes. The problems became more frequent as planes became faster but eventually new designs were able to deal with the problems. Another

---

71 The most prominent exception to this statement was, of course, the P-51 during World War II which was conceived, designed and built (without the engine) in less than four months. Even though the builder, North American Aviation, had never before built a fighter, its creation was generally considered the best propeller-driven fighter of World War II. Moreover it had very few model changes during its service life. Only the P-51B and the P-51D models were used, the latter being by far the largest model run.

not previously seen serious problem plagued the next phase of flight. The fighter race with the Soviet Union had, after some difficulty, gone beyond the speed of sound but the aircraft manufacturers were not out of the woods yet. Some of their models defied the slide rules (there being no useful design computers at that time) and refused to perform as the engineers had predicted. Eventually the "area rule" became understood and another hurdle to supersonic flight was cleared. In addition to the usual problems involved in designing cutting edge aircraft these two serious and complicated issues had to be dealt with, yet new models of high performance aircraft were being put into service very rapidly. It was not that these new and dangerous aircraft might have been beyond the capabilities of the average military pilot although that limit had to be kept in mind during the design process. It is both significant and very sad to realize that the Army Air Force's leading ace in World War II, Richard Bong, was killed while making flight tests on the first operational jet fighter to be built in the United States (the P-80), the United States Air Force's leading ace in the Korean War, William McConnell, was killed while testing an advanced model of the F-86 (the F-86H) and another Air Force Korean War ace, Lonnie R. Moore, was killed testing the F/RF-101 (Voodoo). These aircraft all had ejection seats which should have made it more possible, but by no means certain, that the pilot could escape from an aircraft in trouble. Even the best could be, and were, killed testing new aircraft.

Test pilots of course have a very dangerous job in flying aircraft that may not perform as planned and which have systems on board that have not been perfected. The job of the test pilots is test the various systems of the aircraft to their limits and to bring back detailed reports. That job is made much more difficult by the knowledge that they may be flying the only existing version of the aircraft. There is thus great pressure to bring the aircraft back in reasonable condition so that its problems can be identified and corrected.[72] Otherwise it

---

72 There is extant an unclassified tape made by a chase plane of an early test flight in the F-14 (Tomcat), a Navy fighter with cutting edge technology including movable wings. The F-14 developed problems and started down out of control. In order to try to save the aircraft the crew stayed with it until the plane was

may take as much as a year to produce a replacement to use for further testing, delaying significantly the time before the plane can be put into production. A year's delay at that stage of the Cold War was a huge gap in the thrust and parry escalation of weapons in that war, leading to a temptation to cut short some of the testing so as to make the planes operational at the earliest possible moment.

Consider what the competition with the Soviet Air Force meant. Aircraft designers and builders in the United States were required at least to keep up with Russian aircraft and preferably to exceed them. Making that race even more difficult was the absence of firm data on the Russian aircraft. While most countries try to keep their military weapons secret, the Russians were especially secretive. Some information could be received from defectors and spies but one of the more useful sources was the introduction of new Russian weapons in their Mayday parades which had overflights of new aircraft. Much could be discovered from aircraft flying 1,000 to 2,000 feet over the foreign observers but sometimes the data derived from an overflight could be quite misleading. This was the case when Western observers watched the introduction of one new Soviet aircraft. Pictures were sent back to the West and aeronautical engineers estimated the speed, range and lifting capacity of the plane. The estimates were well off the mark because, among other assumptions, the West assumed the many of the critical parts in the Russian aircraft were made of titanium, a very strong and light metal that is difficult to fabricate. The Russians were well behind the West in the metallurgy of titanium and were thus required to substitute stainless steel, a much heavier but more easily worked metal for some substantial and important structures in their high performance fighters. Although electronics were becoming more important by the year, there was very little that could be discerned about these critical components from pictures beyond the most basic items such as the placement and size of antennae.

In general the West tended to overestimate the Soviet weaponry but in the absence of precise information it was only prudent to

extremely low before they ejected (safely).

assume the worst and to design accordingly. This made the designers' job more difficult, the aircraft more expensive and the test pilots' job more dangerous. In retrospect it became clear how many of the Soviet aircraft had been overestimated in various respects. The results of the literal aircraft race were hurried planning, quick design, fast construction, short flight testing, rapid introduction of new aircraft into squadron service and equally rapid perceived obsolescence. The result was quite often overestimation of the need to turn over aircraft in service. As a not unusual rate of turnover, the author's squadron, the 354th/437th Fighter Interceptor Squadron, was equipped with six quite different fighters in a little more than a decade.[73] In the early years this was difficult for both the air crews and the ground crews because of the time it took for them to become comfortable with the plane. In that period it was not especially wasteful of aircraft because the useful life of the earlier first line jet aircraft was 2,000 flight hours or less. This amounted to an average of about two flights per aircraft per day for two years before the planes would have to be replaced in spite of a usual practice of periodic intensive inspections and returning the aircraft to the manufacturer at the 1,000 hour point for a complete overhaul. As the 2,000 hour period approached the judgment would then have to be made to replace them with some type of aircraft. If more of the same type of aircraft made up the replacements, the aircraft would be easy and relatively cheap to produce and the aircrews and ground crews would not need extensive retraining. On the other hand, the second group of aircraft would not be significantly better than the original ones in an era in which the Soviet Union was improving its aircraft rapidly. If a more recent aircraft were to serve as the replacement, a great deal of training would be necessary for both air and ground crews. The cost of that type of replacement would obviously be much more expensive both because the new aircraft would undoubtedly be more complex and a completely new production line and flight test program would have been necessary. The time from concept to placing the new models in squadron service

---

73 The sequence was from F-51Ds to F-94Cs to F-89Ds to F-89Hs to F-101Bs to F-106s (Delta Dart) or from World War II retreads to second generation supersonics in a little more than a decade.

would be both long and uncertain. The one thing that was certain was that the Soviet air force was improving its aircraft as fast as it was able as were the United States Air Force and Navy.

While the contest among the Russians, the British and the Americans to determine how to stop the enemy long-range bombers armed with atomic weapons seemed at the time to be the most important problem of the military forces of all three countries, it appeared clear to all parties that there was probably no defense adequate to destroy substantially all of an incoming raid of intercontinental strategic bombers. The only defense was an offence in return, effectively producing a standoff. That situation might have pleased most parties but all had realized that someone might break the standoff, either by mistake or intentionally, producing full-scale nuclear war with, in all probability, everyone losing. Although the United States had four years of monopoly of nuclear weapons for the period after it had won the armament race to atomic bombs in 1945, it had not used that power against the Soviet Union. In 1949 when the Russians had exploded their first atomic bomb the atomic armament race was tied and a frantic arms race began. The arms race encompassed both the number of atomic weapons in the arsenals of the contending powers and the types and number of delivery systems for those weapons.

In terms of available delivery systems initially there was only one practical military type of such a system – delivery by aircraft. Since the early atomic bombs were quite heavy, on the order of four or five tons, large bombers were the likely carriers. There was some thought that the Soviet Union might attempt to smuggle an atomic bomb into the United States by ship or truck but, at least in retrospect, that seemed unlikely. Even if the bomb were not discovered before being exploded and if a crew could be found to deliver such a weapon, the Soviet government would have lost precise control of if and when the detonation of the bomb would happen.

The possibility of an atomic attack on the United States created a high level of panic among civilians in the United States during the fifties.

Public buildings were designated as air raid shelters, schools practiced air raid drills and people started to build air raid shelters in their back yards. People who were in school in that era still remember the drill that said if they saw a very bright light they should "drop and cover" to provide some protection from an atomic blast. Later, particularly after the hydrogen bomb had been developed, people became somewhat more realistic and recognized that there was not much that they could do to protect themselves from the blast of an atomic weapon. The air raid shelters then became potentially more useful as fallout shelters and, as is probably usual in periods of extended threat, the initial panic wore off. This was not because the risk has declined but rather because there seems to be a limit to the period of time one can stay worked up over a long-term risk regardless of how severe that risk is.

The United States armed forces, and initially particularly the United States Air Force, had the difficult job of trying to protect the country from Soviet attacks with atomic weapons. There were two aspects to the job. One was to attempt to shoot down incoming Soviet bombers before they could drop their bombs. Although the Air Defense Command had state-of-the-art all-weather fighters which were kept up to date as described earlier, the chances of fighters or anti-aircraft rockets destroying most of the incoming bombers were quite remote. In World War II defenses against strategic bombers that destroyed 10% of the attackers were considered to have done well. Since the conventional bombing was then not likely to be particularly accurate, it was usually necessary to make a number of raids in order to destroy a target. A 10% attrition rate would thus not permit the attacking force to continue to try to destroy the target without destroying itself. Atomic bombs were different. The ratio could have been reversed. If 90% of the bombing force had been destroyed before dropping their bombs, the attack would still have been entirely successful because of the enormous damage that would have resulted from those atomic and hydrogen bombs dropped by the few surviving bombers. The second aspect of the defense against atomic attack was the threat of responding in kind by bombing the Soviet Union with atomic and hydrogen bombs. It was this threat of mutual destruction by strategic bombing that seemed to be the restraining factor during the heavily armed peace for the two decades after the end of World War II.

While the world did not need two more techniques for self-destruction, it found itself with them. The first was a great advance over the German V-2 but was a similar weapon. While the V-2 had a range of only a few hundred miles it was a very fast true ballistic missile. The V-2 was launched from the vertical position with its extremely powerful liquid-fueled engine carrying it up to a distance of about 200 miles under gyroscopic direction. When the engine cut off after about one minute of operation, the missile continued on its preset course arcing down to strike the ground at high supersonic speed and to set off its warhead. There was no way to stop or even to redirect the V-2 once it had been launched. After the end of the war both the Russians and the Americans obtained the German material on ballistic missiles as well as a number of completed missiles. They both started work on an arms race using much more advanced ballistic missiles, culminating in the terrifying intercontinental ballistic missiles with one or multiple atomic warheads and the range to cover the distance from the Soviet Union to the United States or vice versa in about half an hour. The missiles were generally housed in what were called silos but were in fact underground launching sites that were often "hardened" against any damage from an enemy attack short of a direct atomic hit on the installation. This was a much more dangerous situation than that which existed with strategic bombers armed with atomic bombs. The bombers could be put on a war footing and launched with atomic weapons toward the enemy's strategic targets with at least the theoretical option on the part of their commander to recall the strike by coded radio messages if the situation had changed. The dangerous links in this system were the possibilities that a recall of the strike force would not be received, would be misinterpreted or would have been made by the enemy. While these events never happened they provided scenarios that were used in books and movies throughout the Cold War and were realistic models for an atomic war between the United States and the Soviet Union.

Frightening as were the potentially non-stoppable attacks by intercontinental ballistic missiles there was worse yet to come. At the end of World War II submarines were similar but not identical to the submarines that had started the war. Germany in particular had improved the range and the ability to stay underwater of some of its submarines but they were still not true submarines in the sense of spending substantially all of their time under water. Their speed under water was still much slower than their speed on the surface and, to make matters worse, the faster they tried to travel under water the faster they used up their battery power and the shorter the amount of time they could stay submerged. The only way they had to recharge their batteries was to surface and turn on their diesel engines. It might have been possible to launch a V-1 type weapon from a surfaced submarine close to land. If it had been possible to build an atomic bomb small enough and light enough to be fitted into the nose of that V-1 type of cruise weapon then it might have been possible to use the combination in submarines. Of course making the bomb large enough to produce an atomic explosion yet small and light enough to be delivered in a cruise missile in the early days of the nuclear standoff would probably have emitted sufficient radiation in the delivery submarine to endanger the whole crew. By the latter days of the nuclear standoff the Soviet navy did have nuclear-tipped torpedoes but not without some serious incidents.

Ten years after the end of World War II the United States Navy put into service what was then by far the most advanced submarine in the world, USS *Nautilus*. She was powered entirely by atomic energy and had a system that purified and recirculated the air in the submarine so efficiently that the submarine could be sealed up at the beginning of a voyage and not be resupplied with air until the crew left her months later at the end of a long cruise. While in the latter days of World War II Germany had developed a system for taking on air to a submerged submarine this was only a small step in the right direction. The German invention was called the snorkel. It enabled a submarine traveling at periscope depth to extend a tube to the surface of the sea and draw down air both for the crew and for the diesel engines without the submarine having to surface. The snorkel was an important advancement in submarine technology but the metal snorkel was above the water and thus was detectable by radar. Other disadvantages of the snorkel were that the submarine would have to be traveling at a very shallow depth to use it and, perhaps most importantly, it was very hard on the crew. The snorkel had a device for shutting it down quickly when waves broke over the air intake. Since the snorkel was supplying air for both the crew and the engines, when it shut down the engines in order to keep running had to draw the necessary air from inside the boat, creating a partial vacuum in the boat. These rapid barometric pressure changes produced serious physiological effects on the crew and stresses on the equipment.

With atomic power requiring no air and the crew having renewable air at normal atmospheric pressure the true submarine that submariners had been hoping for had finally been born and an important armament race had been won by the United States. Had the Cold War turned at hot at that time the United States would have had a great advantage. But the Cold War stayed cold and the Soviet Navy worked very rapidly, although not always very carefully, to try to catch up. The accident record of the United States Navy and that of the Soviet Navy with respect to atomic powered submarines may not be complete in the published records but what has been published demonstrates clearly the very serious problems that the Soviet Navy has had with its atomic powered submarines. The United States Navy has acknowledged the loss of two atomic submarines, USS *Thresher* and USS *Scorpion*. The cause of the loss of the former was apparently a failure of the pressure hull while that of the latter is unknown but has been attributed to possible external explosions by some.[74] On the other hand the Soviet Navy has had what could only be described as an appalling accident rate with its atomic submarines. Beginning after a serious radiation leak on SSN *K-8* in October 1960 (the ship survived) the following events

---

74 See *Navy Press Release* dated 26 Oct 1993. The language is very carefully crafted with respect to implosions (as might have happened if her pressure hull had failed) and explosions (as might have happened if she had been torpedoed).

occurred causing damage or loss of a nuclear-powered submarine or radiation injuries to the crew:

July 1961 Radiation leak in SSBN *K-19* with many deaths. The ship survived.

1965 Reactor accident in port. The ship survived.

September 1967 *K-3* Fire at sea with many deaths. The ship survived.

May 1968 *K-27* Accident in the reactor with deaths. The ship survived.

April 1970 *K-8* sinks.

Alpha class had a reactor meltdown.

February 1972 SSBN *K-19* had another reactor accident with many deaths.

September 1977 SSBN *K-171* had to dispose of a nuclear warhead at sea.

December 1978 SSBN *K-171* had a reactor failure with deaths

August 1980 SSN project 659 had a fire with deaths.

November 1980 *K-162* power surge ashore with damage to reactor.

June 1983 SSGN *K-429* sank with damage to missile tubes, 16 deaths.

June 1984 SSGN *K-131* on board fire with deaths.

August 1985 SSGN *K-431* explosion and fire with deaths.

October 1986 *K-219* had a missile explosion and fire with deaths.

April 1989 *K-278* had a fire and sank with many deaths

August 2000 SSGN *K-141* exploded and sank, 118 deaths.[75]

---

75 This list of incidents came from Huchthausen, *K-19 The Widowmaker* (2002), pp. 213-21. These are by no means the only incidents Capt. Huchthausen cited involving the Soviet Navy's nuclear submarines during the period. Many incidents which appeared not to be related to nuclear propulsion or did not involve casualties have been omitted from the list.

There were about this many more events involving the Soviet nuclear navy during the same period but the additional ones do not seem to have been closely connected to the nuclear power plant although some did involve torpedoes with nuclear warheads.

It would be fair to say that, in spite of the United States winning the armament race with USS *Nautilus,* the arms race which followed was a draw. The draw did have its place in the "assured mutual destruction" scenario which dominated at least the American thinking throughout the Cold War. The result was that by the mid-1970s both the Soviet Union and the United States had placed in service their strategic bombers armed with atomic weapons and their land-based intercontinental ballistic missiles armed with atomic warheads. Each side had its weapons aimed at the other. Backing up this appalling amount of potential destruction, much of which was available with a delivery time of about a half hour were two fleets of nuclear submarines, each capable of rapidly launching a dozen or more intermediate range ballistic missiles at targets within their range. As a consequence of these faster delivery systems being in place to supplement or even to supercede the subsonic strategic bombers, the urgency of having fighter aircraft replaced every few years with faster and longer ranged aircrft was greatly diminished as were the fleets of those subsonic strategic bombers. It might seem that the intercontinental and long-range ballistic missiles and medium-range ballistic submarine launched ballistic missiles should have been an adequate determent on both sides, outmoding the strategic bombers and causing them to be removed from each country's arsenal. Bomber-carried atomic weapons, however, did retain the distinct advantage of being able to be recalled before delivery if the crisis mitigated while the bombers were in flight toward their enemy.

As a result of the changed emphasis away from strategic bombers carrying atomic weapons, the United States Navy and the United States Air Force were able break their frantic development cycle and to design and build at some leisure a quartet of extraordinary fighters designed to serve in a tactical capacity not for several years but rather for several decades. The result was the appearance into squadron service in the

70s of the Navy's F-14 and F/A 18 (Hornet) and the Air Force's F-15 (Eagle) and F-16 (Fighting Falcon). As of the date of this book three of these planes were still in first-line service with the United States military. The fourth, the F-14, was retired in 2006 not because it had become uncompetitive with respect to the aircraft of potential enemies but only because the maintenance costs of keeping the aircraft on active duty had become too high. This was in large measure because of its extraordinary electronics and probably more importantly because of its moveable wings.[76] This decision was reinforced by the recognition that our then potential enemies did not have aircraft that required something as effective as the F-14 to oppose them. Between the mid-seventies and 2006 those four United States fighters were the class of the world, an extraordinary length of time for supremacy when compared to less than a year for World War I fighters, perhaps two years of service on average for World War II fighters and probably about the same for the first half of the Cold War. While it might seem curious that the development time for most of the World War II and early Cold War fighters was about the same even though the later fighters were much more complex. The reason, of course, was the arms race with the Soviet Union. As mentioned earlier, for many of the early Cold War aircraft the development time was less than it should have been. If it had been known that there would not have been direct combat between the two superpowers more development time could have been devoted to fewer aircraft models and the aircraft would have been safer, better and cheaper but, given the state of the confrontation between the Soviet Union and United States, aircraft were being designed, built and retired at about the same rate as had been the case since the beginning of World War II. This high turnover rate of aircraft had an enormous effect on the air forces and military expenditures of both countries.

The point of the foregoing is to establish the not very surprising fact that the time spent on the development of particular military

---

76   The moveable wing on the F-14 was necessary because the aircraft needed a straight wing for the low speed necessary for aircraft carrier landings and takeoffs and a swept wing for the very high top speed necessary to compete with enemy aircraft threatening the fleet.

weapons has been fairly constant over the last two centuries as has been the response to those developments. There have been exceptions of very accelerated developments and/or responses, perhaps most notably in the cases of *La Gloire* and *Warrior* in the mid-nineteenth century and the continual rapid evolution of aircraft during World War I. In general, however, there has been at least a two to four year time for conception, planning and initial construction of many new military weapons followed by a test period of some duration. To the extent that greater time was needed, the new idea was usually outmoded by events and dropped, perhaps to be replaced by a copy or an advanced version of an enemy's developed weapon.

We now come to a weapon the development time alone of which exceeded by far the total development and service time of many, perhaps most, of the military weapons of the twentieth century. It is, of course, the Osprey (fabricated) but first we shall have a brief review of its namesake.

Osprey (feathered)

We can now return to our starting point, ospreys. The feathered osprey is a handsome bird. It is categorized as a raptor from the Latin word for plunderer. It has curved talons, a curved beak and is a type of hawk. In fact one of the osprey's common names is "fish hawk." It flies and glides very well, in large measure because its wingspread as an adult approximates six feet while its weight as a full-grown bird is only about four pounds. As is the case with most birds, its large bones are hollow. Notwithstanding these indications of fragility the osprey is supposed to be the only raptor which dives full speed, sometimes as fast as 40 miles per hour, into the water to catch the fish that make up most of its diet. Ospreys usually mate for life and build rather messy nests of branches in the forks of trees, on telephone poles and on platforms set on top of poles erected for the purpose. Until the middle of the twentieth century ospreys were well distributed in areas with a supply of fish of a size that ospreys could catch and carry away to their nests.

The middle of the twentieth century created a problem that could have eliminated the ospreys. The problem was an insecticide. That insecticide had been used during World War II to control insects bearing serious diseases like malaria, yellow fever and encephalitis, particularly in the South Pacific. The insecticide was dichlorodiphenyltrichloroethane, for obvious reasons almost always abbreviated to DDT. Before it was tried in the field there had been serious concerns about possible side effects from its use. Testing was done and, to the relief of all, the DDT that reached the ground turned into harmless substances quite quickly. DDT did a good job during the war of controlling insects and thus insect-borne diseases. After the war DDT was widely used in the United States and it was equally effective here, so much so that seemed to many to be a miracle compound. Gradually, however, it appeared as though DDT was having a serious impact on the environment, most notably on the eggs of birds. DDT in the birds' system caused the birds' eggs to have thinner shells than normal and thus were more fragile. When nesting birds sat on the eggs they tended to break. The populations of certain birds declined precipitately until there was concern that some species would disappear entirely. Rachel Carson in her book *Silent Spring* pointed out the effect of DDT-like compounds on the environment. In 1972 the Environmental Protection Agency was created and DDT was banned. The endangered species, including ospreys, began to recover slowly. It turned out that the early research on DDT was accurate as far as it had gone; DDT did decompose into harmless elements on the ground. What had not been properly understood was that the insects that were killed by the DDT sprays did not always or even often decompose on the ground. They were generally eaten by other insects, by birds or by fish. The DDT originally in the bodies of the killed insects was transferred intact up the food chain from prey to predator and thus, over time, built up its concentration in the final predator producing, among other things, thin-shelled eggs in egg-laying animals. After the cause had been identified and DDT had been banned the environment very slowly cleaned itself up. The few remaining ospreys in the eastern United States gradually increased in number toward their historic population to the relief of their many admirers.

It is not then surprising that the name given to a military aircraft could be "Osprey." Predatory, agile and attractive were also characteristics of the Osprey (fabricated). Yet those Ospreys had some other not intended similarities to the Osprey (feathered).

Osprey (fabricated)

The history of human flight did not begin with the legendary flight of Daedalus and Icarus nor was the first aircraft accident the result of structural failure of Icarus' wings by the sun's melting of the wax holding the feathers together. Several thousand years after that mythological flight, human beings did produce a machine for lifting themselves off the ground and returning them safely back to earth. Two Frenchmen gained that honor in the latter part of the eighteenth century. The Montgolfiers noticed that hot air appeared to rise and wondered whether it would be possible to use the force of rising hot air to raise people into the sky. Being extremely cautious they built their first hot air balloon for animals to make sure that air breathing animals could survive in the sky, apparently ignoring the obvious fact that human beings lived quite comfortably in the mountains of France at far higher elevations than the Montgolfier balloons could fly. The experimental flight was a success and human passenger-carrying balloons followed in short order. The heat source for the balloons was straw which was carried aloft in the balloons and fed into the straw fire of the balloon as needed. The flights were necessarily short both because the fuel supply on board was quite limited and because there was no way to control the flight of the balloon. The latter factor required that the balloon had to come down relatively quickly before it drifted away from clear places to land. Additionally there was a serious fire risk with an open flame in the burner and a great expanse of thin cloth in the balloon so staying close to the ground had considerable merit as a safety measure.

While the free hot air balloon was basically a toy with no use except to prove that it was possible for persons to ascend to some heights and return safely to the ground, a vast improvement in balloons was soon to come. The next step in the slow evolution of flight was filling the free balloon with hydrogen gas instead of hot air. Hydrogen is a very light gas, producing a great deal of lift for the volume of gas and the lift continued so long as the hydrogen gas did not leak out of the balloon. On the other hand hydrogen burns and explodes when ignited by as little as a spark of static electricity so it requires extreme care in handling. Nevertheless hydrogen replaced hot air rapidly when it became available. Balloons filled with hydrogen still drifted on the wind but they began to be of some value in mapmaking and exploring. By the time of the American Civil War tethered hydrogen filled balloons were occasionally being put to use by the Union forces to observe actions behind the South's lines in daylight and clear weather. The observer in the balloon could not talk to the personnel on the ground by telephone as was done in later tethered balloons since the telephone had not been invented until well after the Civil War. It would have been possible to pass information from the gondola down to the ground by telegraph as the telegraph was invented before the war but apparently the communications systems of choice were shouting down from the gondola to the ground crew, dropping rocks with notes attached and cranking down the balloon to talk to the observer. Free balloons were also used by the French in connection with the siege of Paris during the Franco-Prussian War in 1870 for both communications and transportation although they did not appear to have helped the French very much in that war. The uses of both tethered balloons and dirigibles in World War I and blimps in World War II has been previously discussed.

The reason for this discussion of lighter-than-air forms of military weapons was to point out that they did not require large areas in which to takeoff and land even though the dirigible and blimp hangers were very large buildings. It is quite advantageous to be able to use flying machines that do not need long runways. It must have been frustrating to early aircraft designers to realize that most birds and flying reptiles had developed zero length takeoff and landing runs although they did tend to land and takeoff into the wind if there was one. The space and construction costs for lighter-than-air machines were much lower than those of airplanes. Things would change dramatically when more heavier-than-air machines entered the stage. By definition conventional heavier-than-air craft cannot just drift up into the air. They must generate enough lift from their wings to counteract the force of gravity in order to rise off the surface. That lift is usually created by the motion of the wings through the air as a result of forward motion caused by engines or moving air although sometimes the forward motion is generated by catapults. This latter system was used by Professor Langley to launch an aircraft even before the Wright brothers flew. Professor Langley proposed to launch his attempt at a heavier-than-air device from a boat in the Potomac by catapult. He wanted to launch it over water so that if it did not work the pilot would not be injured. Obviously he was not aware of the possible danger to the pilot of a rapid impact with water. In any case the light and flimsy structure of his airship was destroyed by the force of the catapult. Also destroyed in the process was Professor Langley's formidable reputation. It was essential in the early years of powered flight that aircraft get up to flying speed as quickly as possible to limit the damage to the plane from the rough ground over which it was rolling. In fact speed across the ground was so critical to the ability of the aircraft to fly that the takeoff run of the Wright Flyer was driven in part by a weight forcing the aircraft along a wooden track; it landed on skids, not wheels, to save weight as well as to limit the damage that the rough ground would cause during a long landing run. Because Professor Langley used a catapult to try to launch his airship before the Wright Brothers flew and because catapults are used today to launch planes from aircraft carriers the aircraft catapult has had a longer life than the airplane.

Once aircraft needed to be able to take off at speeds in excess of the speed of a moderately pedaled bicycle it became necessary to have some kind of smooth open space to allow the aircraft to accelerate to a speed that would create enough lift to launch the aircraft into the air. Once the plane rose from the ground and lost the drag of its wheels on the ground the plane could accelerate and thus generate more lift without more power being necessary. Airfields slowly began to become more standardized. Some were simply more or less smooth large grassy fields. Because it is the speed of the wind over the wings, not the speed of the aircraft over the ground, that determines the lift of the wings, it behooves one to take off and land into the wind. If, for example, one is flying at a site with a 10 mile per hour wind and a speed of 30 miles per hour is necessary to lift the aircraft off the ground and keep it aloft, taking off into the 10 miles per hour wind it would permit the take off to occur at a ground speed of 20 miles per hour and to land into the same wind with a ground speed of 20 miles per hour. Doing this not only makes the takeoff and particularly the landing easier for the pilot, it produces less stress on the aircraft. A large more or less square field has the advantage of allowing aircraft to take off or land exactly into the wind and thus to receive the maximum lift. One disadvantage of the square field is that it it if a 5,000 foot runway is required it would use a square mile of land and would require that there be very limited obstacles near the whole perimeter of the field. Another disadvantage of the square field is that acquiring and paving it would be very expensive as would be the maintenance of the paved surface. On the other hand, a runway or a series of runways would use less land and require less area of height restrictions but, under most circumstances, would provide less lift for the same runway speed. Square fields had an additional advantage for some types of military flying because a number of aircraft could be sent off simultaneously. This type of departure was used by a few countries as late as World War II for defensive fighter scrambles, not so much to get more lift because the takeoffs could be made directly into the wind but rather to be able to assemble a group of aircraft right at takeoff rather than having to devote a considerable amount of flight time to form a formation after a series of individual takeoffs.

Gradually, however, most airfields came to have separate runways with paving to improve the surface and make both takeoffs and landings smoother. Over time the changes in aircraft had an effect on runways. Heavier aircraft needed stronger runways; faster aircraft needed longer runways for both takeoffs and landings. Eventually runways extended to two or three miles in length to handle modern military aircraft.[77] The result of all of this airfield development was that a great deal of

---

77 The record length, at least in the United States, was probably at Edwards Air Force Base in the Mojave Desert. It had a paved runway 15,000 feet long that led into a dry lake which extended the runway by another 9,000 feet. The dry lake was not always dry as a member of the author's squadron found out to his dismay when he made an emergency landing there after a rainstorm.

energy and money was spent on a prime target that was easily put out of action at least temporarily by use of bombs to put craters in the runways. Some sort of flying machine that would not require this type of facility was widely sought and from Spain came an ingenious partial solution. There in 1919 a clever inventor named Juan de la Cierva, after considerable trial and error, perfected a new type of flying machine, the autogyro. The autogyro had a standard appearing fuselage with an empennage, an open cockpit and a propeller in front driven by a standard aircraft engine. What was very strange about the autogyro was that it had no wings. It did have a strange structure attached to the top of the fuselage that looked like the rotor on a helicopter. Since the helicopter was not to be invented for several more decades, the autogyro appeared particularly strange. While one could perhaps think that the overhead rotor would somehow serve in place of wings, when it became clear that the rotor was not powered by the engine the machine was widely ridiculed. The ridicule seemed appropriate until the fifth machine was flown successfully.

Taking off forward, the autogyro would taxi down the runway under the power of the engine driven propeller. As the forward speed built up, the rotor would began to revolve in a mode called autorotation, meaning that the energy causing the rotation was being supplied by the motion of the aircraft through the air and not by a power source within the aircraft. The rotor had no internal source of power. When the rotor was revolving at an appropriate speed it would lift the autogyro off the runway. Between the propeller and the empennage the autogyro could be maneuvered much like a conventional aircraft with one major difference. To land the autogyro the pilot reduced the power of the engine. The autogyro would then slow down causing the rotor to slow down because it was not being moved through the air at a speed that would impart enough energy to the rotor to keep it rotating at adequate speed to hold the altitude. The autogyro would then float down to land more or less vertically on a relatively small piece of land. While the autogyro did not become a major factor in aviation it was an indication that there was room for some type of vertical takeoff and landing vehicle. Perhaps the autogyro would have become a more serious aircraft over time but for subsequent inventions permitting vertical entrance to and exit from ground sites. In any case, however, the autogyro needed runway space both to allow the rotor to reach lifting speed and to permit the autogyro to be moving forward on landing. Without some forward motion the autogyro pilot run the risk of dropping the aircraft very hard on the runway.

It should be noted that, while autogyros were slow-moving aircraft, that was not an inherent condition of autogyros as it was to a large degree in helicopters. Helicopters used their rotors directly to produce lift and indirectly to produce forward or backward motion. Autogyros had their engines attached to tractor propellers pulling the autogyros forward directly. Although the autogyros built in the 1920s and 1930s were generally low-powered and not streamlined, there is reason to believe that they could, in time, have been better powered and streamlined. If so it would have been far easier to make them faster. Helicopters were much more difficult to be adapted for higher speeds. It is also important to note that autogyro rotors were simple to make and install while helicopter rotors and their controls were very complicated. Nevertheless, autogyros would always need runways for takeoff and landing,

Other efforts at vertical takeoffs and landings were tried including unsuccessful propeller and jet driven more or less conventional aircraft with counter rotating propellers or powerful jet engines making vertical takeoffs and landings but the most successful attempt was a modern iteration of a very old idea. More than two millennia ago Chinese children played with toys with rotors on top. Somewhat later Leonardo da Vinci tried his hand at what we now call helicopters but was unable to control the reactive force resulting from the turning of the overhead rotor. It is quite remarkable that between the period of Leonardo and that of the Wright brothers at least as much work seems to have been done by people on helicopters than was done in the same period on fixed wing aircraft. In the twentieth century developments on potential helicopters continued but at a slow pace compared to the explosion of work on fixed wing aircraft. None the less, work on prototypes continued in many European countries. France, Italy, the Netherlands and Germany were active sites of attempts at vertical lift aircraft. Initially progress was measured by very small increments in distance, altitude, lifting capacity and duration, but by the late nineteen thirties Folke-Wolf in Germany actually went into the production of a few helicopters which were used to a minor degree in World War II. Those helicopters were of the dual overhead rotor type. In the meantime LePage and Sikorsky in the United States were making their own designs for helicopters. LePage was working on a form of helicopter much like Folke-Wolf's while Sikorsky preferred a single overhead rotor with a small vertical rotor in the rear to counteract the torque of the main rotor, thus solving Leonardo's problem. Sikorsky's system prevailed and he received a contract from the United States Army for 100 of his machines which were used sparingly in World War II.

While the helicopter looks much like an autogyro it is important to recognize the differences. In an autogyro the rotor, while obviously a crucial component of the craft, is simply a large fan keeping the autogryo in the air by almost parasitic motion. Other components, the propeller and the empennage, control the flight of the craft. Helicopters on the other hand receive all of their maneuvering directions via the flight controls to the rotor. Because the helicopter rotor controls almost all of the flight activities it has to be, and is, a very sophisticated device. It produced the maneuvering that inventors had been striving for over centuries and the result is an incredibly versatile machine that, among other advantages, used virtually no space on the ground. Naturally there is a downside to the helicopter. In order to achieve the ability to move vertically the helicopter is not very efficient in either speed or in fuel consumption while moving horizontally under the power of the overhead rotor.

Sikorsky stayed in the helicopter manufacturing business after World War II. Bell Aircraft also entered the field and manufactured a great many small single rotor helicopters. A number of other companies also entered the field after the war with special purpose machines. The helicopter became an important factor in aviation, both civilian and military, for the second half of the twentieth century beginning with its wide and well publicized use in the Korean War. These developments did not, however, reduce the need for full sized airports with two mile long runways and large expanses of concrete and asphalt. The helicopters became much more a supplement to conventional aircraft than a substitute for them. There were, of course, some jobs that could only be done by helicopters, medical evacuations for example. The alternatives for such jobs were various types of surface transportation, not other forms of aviation. Furthermore, as commercial aircraft evolved during this period they required even greater ground space. The transition from propeller driven aircraft first to turboprop aircraft and then to pure jets required progressively longer and stronger runways and the increase in air traffic tended to cause additional airports to be built. Parallel runways were often added to existing airports to handle the increased traffic. All of these developments were both very expensive and very space consuming. What was needed was a larger and faster vertical takeoff and landing aircraft, preferably one that needed no airport at all.

In the early 1980s work was begun on an aircraft that to fill some of these requirements by using elements of conventional aircraft, helicopters and autogyros. It was called the Osprey and initially was a United States Army project. Not far into the project it was realized that the aircraft would probably be more useful to the United States Marines Corps. The Marine Corps, along with the United States Navy, had an additional and difficult requirement to be able to lift personnel and material off ships at sea and deliver those cargos where needed quickly and vertically in the absence of airfields. As a result the Navy and the Marine Corps took over the leadership of the project. The Osprey (V-22) was the result of those requirements after what must have been the longest gestation period in military aircraft history, being two and one half times the period taken to decide, develop and execute a plan to place a man on the moon and return him safely to the earth. The Osprey was the clear winner in its armament race but, so far as is known publicly there were no other participants and there might well be an argument that the Osprey was not so different or so advanced that it qualified as a candidate for an armament race notwithstanding the extraordinary length of time that it took to develop it. Given the development cost of the Osprey it is not surprising that no other country seemed to be competing. The October 8, 2007, issue of *TIME* had on its cover a picture of the V-22 and a description saying

> **"It's unsafe.**
> **It can't shoot straight.**
> **It's already cost**
> **30 lives and $20 billion.**
> **And now it's headed for**
> **Iraq. The long, sad tale**
> **Of the V-22 Osprey"**

The inside heading of the article continues in the same vein.

> "Flying Shame
> After an investment of $20 billion,
> 25 years and 30 lives, the V-22
> Osprey arrives in Iraq to make
> its combat debut – lacking both
> firepower and the ability to land
> safely if it loses power at low
> altitudes. A TIME investigation
> by Mark Thompson"

The Osprey was thought by most to be a completely new idea for aircraft. It was not. Efforts have been made for the last sixty years to reduce and/or eliminate the need for runways for takeoffs and landings. In the early 1950s zero length launchers for fighters were tried. State of the art fighters were placed on portable launching ramps and launched by very powerful, brief duration rockets. The system never got beyond the testing stage because, among other problems, the transition from rocket power to engine power was difficult for the pilot given the very high G forces of the starting and stopping of the rocket boost. This system, even if it had been more successful as a launching device, would still have required a full-length runway for landings. Various types of vertical launching and recovering aircraft had also been tried. Several aircraft manufacturers in the United States did extensive work on the concept. The Convair XFY-1 (Pogo)[78] was a small one-person plane delta winged aircraft powered by a turboprop engine driving counterrotating propellers which would lift the aircraft from its vertical stance. At some relatively low altitude the plane could then be nosed down to a more or less level flight. At the end of the flight the plane would lift the nose to a vertical position and reduce the engine power to a level that would not support the plane at its altitude and it would gradually sink down backwards to the ground for a landing.

At more or less the same time Lockheed was developing its own version of a tail sitter, the XFV-1 (Salmon). It appeared to be quite similar to the XFY-1 including the counterrotating propellers except that it was straight winged not swept wing. It also differed in that it never was able to take off vertically.

The final early tailsitter was built by Ryan. It was called the X-13 and made its first vertical takeoff in 1957. Its design reverted back to that of the Convair XFY-1 in that its wing was a delta shape but its main addition to the tailsitter clan was that it was powered by a pure jet and not an internal combustion or a jet powered set of propellers. It seemed to have had better flight characteristics than its two predecessors but, like all of the tailsitters, it was plagued by the problem of how to back down into the necessary vertical landing.

It turned out that while the vertical takeoff was difficult but possible, safely landing seemed to be impossible. There were at least three reasons for that. First, it was very dangerous to land in any sort of a wind both because the pilot would have great difficulty in landing where it was intended to be, coupled with the risk that the aircraft might topple over if it were moving sideways when it touched down. Second, if there were any problems with the engine when the aircraft

---

78 Notwithstanding the award of the nickname Pogo to the XFY-1, all of the "tailsitters" seemed to answer to the name of Pogo or Pogostick.

was moving backwards there could be no recovery of the type that was possible in a vertical takeoff when the aircraft was moving forward and might be able to glide to a belly landing or even fly if some of the engine power was left. Third, in spite of the efforts of the manufacturers a satisfactory position for the pilot to handle both vertical and horizontal flight comfortably was never found. Although the potential of engine failure while landing and the problem of positioning the pilot to be able to handle both vertical and horizontal flight well were difficult, perhaps impossible issues, it might seem that the wind drift problem could have been solved or at least ameliorated. Some sort of fencing, perhaps twice the height of the aircraft, could reduce considerably the wind close to the ground. The problems with this approach are at least two. First, the pilot would have a very small target in which to land but secondly, and probably more importantly, the flexibility of availability of landing sites would be severely limited. That flexibility is one of the major advantages of a VTOL. Efforts to develop aircraft in this direction were abandoned.

Somewhat later, but still well ahead of the Osprey, there were other efforts at VTOL aircraft more along the lines of the Osprey. That is to say that the aircraft remained in a horizontal position in their landing and taking off stages by the use of engines with propellers in wingtip nacelles which could be rotated from the horizontal to the vertical. Not surprisingly Bell Aircraft (one member of the manufacturing team of the Osprey) was in the forefront of this line of experimental aircraft with the XV-15 which had two turboshaft engines driving larger than usual propellers. The XV-15 was quite successful in the period after its first flight in 1977 and Bell was also successful with a variation of the propellers in an earlier attempt (the X-22) using four turboshafts with the propellers surrounded by ducts to control the airflow. The aircraft was described as looking "like four rubbish bins attached to a fuselage blundering through the sky"[79] but the tilt rotor made the X-22A a very useful preamble to the V-22s.

---

79 Winchester, *Concept Aircraft* (2005), p. 40.

Subsequent to these efforts an actual vertical takeoff and landing aircraft was perfected. The British Harrier (AV-83) (Harrier II in United States Marine Corps terminology) jet-powered ground attack fighter solved some of the vertical takeoff and landing problems by using a powerful jet engine with vectored thrust, allowing the Harrier to take off and land in a horizontal position while moving vertically. This made the transition to and from level flight much easier. The problem with the Harrier was that its engine thrust was only slightly more than the weight of the aircraft, limiting severely the amount of ordinance and fuel that the plane could lift vertically. By using a brief horizontal takeoff run, the amount of fuel and ordinance that could be carried was increased and the landing could still be made vertically if the ordinance were jettisoned or used or if enough of the Harrier's fuel had been burned to bring the aircraft's weight down. That is not to say that the Harriers could not take off vertically if necessary. They could but their payload, of ordinance for instance, would be greatly limited if it had to be lifted vertically. The available takeoff load could be considerably increased by installing an upward curve at the end of that short runway (a "ski jump"). The use of this technique resulted in a change in the label on the Harrier II from VTOL (Vertical Take Off and Landing) to STOVL (Short Take Off and Vertical Landing). The Harrier II will be replaced in United States service, beginning in 2012, by the Lockheed Martin F-35B (Lightning II) which will also be labeled as an STOVL rather than a VTOL.

In some ways the most unusual predecessor of the Osprey was an extraordinary aircraft developed by Bell Aircraft in 1955. It was called by Bell the XF-109 in the Air Force version and the XF3L in the Navy version.[80] This project was begun half a century before the Osprey was completed and looked much like a conventional straight high-winged

---

80 These identifying designations, while bestowed by Bell on the projects, apparently were never confirmed by the military even though they were in the proper form and sequence. On the other hand, they were never otherwise used by the military in the formal lists as designations for other aircraft. The result is that these designation are routinely still used to describe the aircraft. See Jones, *U.S. Fighters* (1975), pp. 293-95.

twin engine aircraft except that it had eight jet engines, two on each wing tip in nacelles, two in the rear of the fuselage and two mounted vertically in the fuselage. For vertical flight the two vertical engines in the fuselage were used together with the four engines in the nacelles which for takeoff were pointed up. Once in the air the nacelles were to be rotated in order to be aligned with the fuselage, the vertical engines were shut down and the engines in the tail were started up. For landing the takeoff configuration of the engines would be used except that the power would of course be reduced. The nacelles could be rotated 10 degrees beyond the vertical, allowing the aircraft to back up a bit while in the air. The engines were conventional General Electric models each with a dry power of about 2,600 pounds of thrust which could be augmented to about 3,800 pounds of thrust in afterburner. The idea of using so many small engines in an era in which reliable jet engines in the 10,000 to 15,000 pound range were available seems strange unless the small size of the XF-109 would not permit any larger engines to be installed. The mockup of the plane showed it to be a very sleek design, looking more like a refugee from a *Star Wars* movie than a design from an aircraft manufacturer of the mid-1950s. Eight engine aircraft were not unheard of at the time and in fact were built in the late 1940s and 1950s but those aircraft were much larger than the XF-109. The B-52, which came into service in 1955, had in its first production model eight P&W J57 9,700 pound thrust jet engines and the B-36 which was going out of service at the same time had a total of ten engines, six P&W R-3640 reciprocating engines in a pusher configuration and four GE J47 jet engines. Both aircraft carried on-board engineers for the engines.[81] It was not clear why the XF-109 was abandoned after intensive engineering studies and a full-size mockup but it might have been simply that there was too much new technology in general or to be able to be handled by one person.

The Osprey, like the X-15 before it, also looks much like a conventional straight high-winged twin engine transport except that the engines are located in the wing tips and have very much larger

81   But the B-47 from the late 1940s had six jet engines and carried only two pilots and a navigator/bombardier.

propellers. The concept behind the aircraft is that the Osprey can turn the engine nacelles on the wing tips to a vertical position which would allow the propellers to generate upward thrust to lift the aircraft vertically. The rotors would turn in opposite directions which would have no effect on the amount of lifting power available but would serve to reduce substantially the torque reaction to the rotation of the rotors in the overhead position. The Osprey would then work much as the larger models of the conventional overhead powered twin rotor helicopters had been operating for decades. When the Osprey had gained sufficient altitude, the engine nacelles would be rotated 90 degrees forward which would place them in the usual position for tractor propellers on more conventional aircraft. The rotors lift would be rotated forward as thrust; lift would then be developed by the resulting forward motion of the aircraft causing air to move over the wings and to generate lift in the conventional way. This direct forward thrust producing lift by the airfoil in the wings was a far more effective way of generating forward motion and lift than the variable rotor used by conventional helicopters. The Osprey was thus faster as well as being larger than most of the earlier types of twin rotor helicopters. The engineers designing the Osprey created a system which would allow either of the engines to drive both rotors in the event of the other engine not functioning. Single engine flight would not be very fast but would allow the Osprey to get away. This was an important consideration but it was usual, although not universal, for twin engine military aircraft. The Osprey could not function with both engines out but neither could any other twin engine aircraft.

It probably does not surprise the reader to be told that a twin engine aircraft does not work well if both of its engines are inoperative. One might wonder that the *TIME* article makes such a point of this "failing" although in one sense *TIME*'s position might not be quite so strange. Helicopters for decades have been able to do what was somewhat the equivalent of a glide of a conventional aircraft which had suffered total engine failure. So long as there was an area suitable for landing, even for a crash landing and there was reasonably good weather, the pilot of a conventional aircraft with a dead engine or engines could usually manage to get his craft on the ground without serious damage to the occupants, provided always that the pilot had the ability to operate the control surfaces (ailerons, elevators, rudders and flaps) with the engine(s) inoperative. The aircraft, of course, might be seriously damaged or destroyed. The pilot of a conventional helicopter could do something quite similar. Assuming that given whatever had caused the engine to fail would still allow the rotor to turn, the rotor would impart some lift to the helicopter. The pilot could disengage the rotor from the engine, allowing it to spin freely. As the helicopter dropped straight down, that motion would cause the now freewheeling rotor to spin rather like the rotor on an autogyro, imparting some lift to the helicopter and thus significantly reducing the rate of descent and limiting the damage to the helicopter and its occupants that would occur when the helicopter hit the surface. This condition is called autorotation. In fact it for every helicopter it can be calculated just how much the descent will be slowed after dropping different distances. The landing will not be gentle and the contact with the ground would probably do serious damage to the helicopter but if the altitude if the altitude is high enough the crew would probably be able to walk away from the landing. The ability to walk away from an aircraft which has just arrived on the ground regardless of the form of arrival and/or the condition of the aircraft has, for decades, been an aviator's facetious description of a successful landing. From perhaps 40 or 50 feet in the air (individual helicopters will have different distances) down to the ground the crash would probably be survivable even though there would not be much if any braking effect from autorotation. Over that height and up to an altitude high enough to enable the fall to impart sufficient energy to the freewheeling rotor to allow it to act as a brake on the falling helicopter and slow its rate of descent to a survivable speed the helicopter would crash and the occupants would probably not survive. The "high enough" altitude would probably be on the order of 400 feet or more. That altitude for each helicopter model forms the top of what is sometimes called the "Dead Man Zone," the bottom being the projected maximum survival altitude of a helicopter with a dead engine and no adequate autorotation yet. Because most helicopters had such a zone with survivable zones above and below it although was usually it very limited, the fact that the Osprey had a possible Dead Man Zone of at least five times the height of a typical helicopter's Dead Man Zone and covered a large part of the likely flight altitudes in which the Osprey would be operating in combat zones gives some credence to *TIME*'s position on its non-survivability.

It should be noted that one comment on autorotation in the *TIME* article needs to be viewed with some skepticism. It said that "up to 90% of the helicopters lost in the Vietnam War" were trying to land when hit and "about half" were able to land by autorotation. First, these are rather fuzzy statistics. More importantly, almost all of the helicopters in Vietnam were single engine. Any loss of that engine meant that the helicopter would come down quickly, with autorotation if possible. The Osprey has two engines, either one of which is adequate to keep the aircraft flying. It would be reasonable to suggest that while an Osprey's chances of making an autorotation landing successfully was much less than those of a conventional helicopter of the types flown in Vietnam, the chances of the Osprey losing both engines through battle damage would be much less than the chances of a Vietnam-era helicopter losing its only engine through battle damage. The risks of being unable to control the damaged craft might well thus be approximately the same for Vietnam War helicopters and Ospreys. The complications of engineering the interconnecting of the two rotors for single engine operation were quite significant but turned out to be solvable. Nonetheless the abilities of the Osprey would be severely limited during periods of single engine operation. Of course any time twin engine aircraft are operating on one engine they have much reduced capabilities although they generally have the ability to stay airborne especially if some cargo is jettisoned. In fact, by virtue of the Osprey's wing it probably has better survival possibilities than a conventional twin engine helicopter since it would be capable of some degree of gliding. An unknown factor in all of this emergency activity is the amount of control the pilot would have over the flight control surfaces during a total absence of engine power. If there were direct wire linkages from the pilot's controls to the rudders, the elevators and the ailerons, those control surfaces would probably be usable. Such systems have been used in combat aircraft, among others the author's F-94C. It worked but it required great effort on the part of the pilot. Because even the maximum possible effort without hydraulic assistance could only move the control surfaces a small amount, a great deal of space for any maneuvers was needed. With all engine power lost in that aircraft and the aircraft gliding down with the hydraulic boost on the flight controls not functioning (which would of course be the case with a dead engine) there was very little movement possible in the control surfaces. Aileron function in such conditions was so limited that a 360 degree turn took 7,500 feet of altitude. Given the relatively low altitudes at which the Osprey would likely be flying only very limited maneuvers would be possible with such a system. While detailed information on the control linkages is classified so far as the author is aware, it is very likely that the control surfaces are controlled hydraulically. Total engine failure would probably cause a loss of flight controls unless a backup mechanical system was installed as is the case with automobile brakes or there were a backup auxiliary hydraulic system available.

Another complaint listed by *TIME* also may have some merit. The Osprey was originally intended to be equipped with a .50 caliber machine gun mounted to fire forward and to be remotely controlled by the pilot. The final version of the Osprey has, as its only automatic weapon, a .30 caliber machinegun manually operated and firing only to the rear. While one could argue the case for a forward firing weapon to clear a landing zone or for an aft firing one to protect an extractive operation, there is no question that a .50 machinegun is a far more powerful weapon than a .30 caliber machinegun.[82] The firing direction, aft or forward, is clearly a matter of choice. That choice, however, was greatly influenced not so much by the position of the gun, the caliber of the bullets nor the field of fire but rather by the method of aiming

---

82   Two-tenths of an inch does not seem like much but in this context it is. The relative hitting power of the .50 caliber round is more than four times that of the .30 caliber round and its range is much longer as well. On the other hand, the .30 caliber weapon is more easily handled manually and its smaller and lighter ammunition allows more rounds to be carried.

and firing the weapon. The rear mounted .30 caliber machine gun is manually aimed and fired by a gunner who could only shoot through the opening created when the loading and unloading ramp in the rear of the Osprey was down. The proposed forward firing .50 caliber machine gun was to have been built into the fuselage and to be fired remotely by a pilot using a very sophisticated gun sight built into the pilot's helmet. It is understandable that one more innovative, expensive and unproved technology may not have been what the Osprey needed during its long development period although there have been recent indications that some sort of forward-firing weapon may appear in later models of the aircraft.

The *TIME* article also makes the point that 30 deaths occurred in the course of the development of the Osprey. This number is correct but in some ways is quite misleading. There were in fact four crashes of Ospreys during the very long development period. It is also worth noting that not only was there was a particularly long and active development period but also that the aircraft incorporated considerable new technology. Four crashes with prototypes would hardly be a surprise with as long a development period as the Osprey. What is very surprising at first glance is the death toll of 30 in those crashes. It is more surprising when one realizes that there were no deaths in one of the crashes. The crash with no fatalities occurred in 1991 as a result of some mistakes made in the aircraft's wiring, causing it to crash from a very low altitude, causing two minor injuries. A year later there was the first fatal crash and a very public one. As a result of a problem with one of the gearboxes a fire started that caused a crash in which all seven of those on board were killed. The crash was at a demonstration flight for members of Congress; not surprisingly it resulted in a significant delay in the program. Eight years later a fully loaded Osprey had a stalled rotor which caused it to roll over and crash, killing all nineteen of the persons on board. Later in the same year, another Osprey had hydraulic failure causing a crash that killed all four on board. The normal crew for an Osprey is three or four, two pilots and one or two engineers. It is also unclear why the risk was taken with personnel unlikely to be able to leave the aircraft to parachute down if indeed they had been issued parachutes for the flight, taught to use them and were flying high enough for the parachutes to deploy. Even had all of these precautions been followed, without ejection seats[83] which the Osprey does not have, it is very difficult to bail out of an aircraft unless it is flying straight and level. Otherwise the motion of the aircraft and the "g" forces likely to be present will make getting through the nearest door or hatch almost impossible in the short time available before a low flying aircraft, like the Osprey, in trouble hits the ground.

The deaths in these Osprey accidents do add up to the 30 deaths reported in *TIME*. It is huge number of fatalities in flight tests on one aircraft and put the Osprey at risk of extermination rather as DDT did for its feathered namesake. Those deaths are a little less shocking when one realizes that they involved only three crashes spread out over almost ten years of the 25 years of the aircraft's development. Why a test flight in an experimental aircraft would have been made with the plane full of men most of whom were not essential to the flight except possibly as ballast is unclear. It does seem as though the large number of fatalities in test flights were due to bad planning of the test flights at least as much as faults in the aircraft. It is also significant that, subsequent to the Osprey becoming operational several years ago, there have been only six incidents with the aircraft, all minor.

Presumably in an effort to mitigate the effect of the upcoming *TIME* article, in August of 2007 Boeing issued a "Backgrounder" entitled *V-22 Osprey*. It described the aircraft and its mission. More importantly, at least from Boeing's point of view in establishing the viability of the aircraft, it listed the customers and their orders and deliveries. The biggest customer and the service with the most Ospreys to be delivered during 2007 was the United States Marine Corps which was to have received three of the first model upgraded eleven newly manufactured MV-22 aircraft. Two CV-22 aircraft were also to be

---

83   Ejection seats were those seats on which aircrew sat which were equipped with rockets to propel their occupants and their parachutes out of the aircraft through canopies or hatches when the seats were fired.

delivered to the Air Force in 2007.[84] At the time of the Backgrounder over 70 Ospreys, mainly Marine, had been delivered and one Marine squadron (VMM-263) had become operational with Ospreys and had been deployed overseas.

In *AIR FORCE* Magazine of May 2008 containing the 2008 USAF Almanac, after reporting that the Air Force had in inventory seven CV-22s out of a planned production of 50 and describing the technical details of the aircraft as follows:

> CV-22 is the designation for the US Special Operations Command variant of the V-22 Osprey. The CV-22 is a multi-engine, dual piloted, self-deployable, medium lift, vertical takeoff and landing (VTOL) tilt rotor aircraft for the conduct of special operations, including nuclear, biological, and chemical (NBC) warfare conditions. It will operate from land bases and from austere forward operating locations as well as air capable ships without reconfiguration or modification. An in-flight refueling capability extends combat mission range when required, and the aircraft will be self-supporting to the maximum practical extent. The CV-22's mission is long-range clandestine penetration of denied areas in adverse weather and low visibility to infiltrate, exfiltrate and resupply SOF [Special Operations Forces],

and goes on to describe the electronics and operational statistics and concludes

> The first operational CV-22 squadron, the 8ᵗʰ SOS [Strategic Operations Squadron] at Hurlburt Field,

---

84 The designation for the Osprey generally is the V-22. The different services have separate designation for Marine, Air Force and Navy equipped versions – the Marine is MV-22, the Air Force is CV-22 and the Navy is HV-22. The differences in these versions reflect the different missions that the three services have in mind for their Ospreys.

Fla., received its first aircraft in January 2007... USAF may place detachments of CV-22s in US European Command and US Pacific Command theaters.

While the Air Force does not evaluate the aircraft described in the Almanac there is nothing derogatory about the Osprey even suggested in the listing. The Air Force seems to be upbeat with the acquisition and deployment of the rest of the 50 Ospreys it has ordered.

What is curious about the two decades plus development period of the Osprey is twofold. First, the time involved was extraordinary. As has been discussed previously, development programs for complicated weapons had gone through time cycles from the end of World War I to date. After that war weapons innovation was almost stopped. A few last efforts were continued on a more or less similar schedule into peacetime, aircraft carriers and tanks, for example. In general, however, weapons development almost ceased after the end of World War I for two principal reasons. First because the winners of the war had huge weapons inventories left over from the war while the losers which had been largely stripped of their weapons had neither the means nor the inclination to engage in rearmament. Secondly, there was still for a decade or so the feeling that that World War I was indeed the War to End All Wars so production of weapons was a waste of money and resources. But during the thirties Germany had resurrected its economy and geared it up for war, causing France and Britain to begin to respond in kind. Japan as well was seeing possible profit in war and acting accordingly. Even the United States and the Soviet Union, in spite of their other internal problems, belatedly realized that it was time to revisit weapons development and production. In designing and building new weapons a design period of several years was common, with the subsequent production time depend upon the size and complexity of the weapon (large naval ships often being good examples of particularly long construction periods).

In contrast, at the conclusion of World War II while the size of the military forces in the United States, Great Britain, France and the

Soviet Union were dramatically reduced after the end of hostilities, their weapons programs, particularly those involving aircraft and submarines, proceeded ahead. Armament races and arms races were still in vogue. In the course of the next 46 years the weapons innovation and production continued at a rapid pace for all parties, particularly those of the United States, the Soviet Union and Great Britain, for all of them knew that another major war was a distinct possibility. It seemed clear to all concerned that a new war would be a fast moving one with little time to prepare for it once it had started. The military establishments in the major powers felt they had to keep their equipment competitive with the other side so the rush to design and produce ever newer weapons for the time when the Cold War would finally heat up. The relevant weapons systems were being updated every bit as rapidly as was the case in World War II although what was relevant changed during the Cold War. Initially World War II type equipment, somewhat improved, was standard. The usual types of aircraft, fighters, bombers and support, were updated and over time were jet powered with much improved electronics. Ships were improved based upon the recent war experience as were tanks and field artillery. As time moved on, major improvements began to appear, initiated by different nations. Also as time moved on the presumed nature of the form of a hot war evolved. The first major change from World War II tactics was the wide use of long range bombers carrying nuclear weapons. In due course long range ballistic missiles based in the Soviet Union and the United States took over from the strategic bombers. In turn, the delivery system of choice later became intermediate range missiles launched from submarines to try to avoid attack from the other side. The 46-year period previously mentioned ended with the collapse of the Soviet Union, taking much of the pressure off weapon development.

Conclusion

As described at the beginning of this book battle records, such as they were, began about thirty-two centuries ago. When, after some considerable period, the records of battles became more complete, the details of the battles began to emerge and the tactics and weapons involved became clearer. Again as suggested earlier weapons changed very slowly for the first thirty of those thirty-two centuries. When the occasional change in tactics occurred, the change could be implemented fairly quickly for the most part. In a possible scenario, a commander loses a battle because of a tactic new to him or he has heard of a new tactic which might be useful to him in a future battle. Let us assume that the new tactic is a single envelopment. The commander will have to train his troops on the elements of the tactic. If he starts with consideration of how the envelopment would be accomplished by his troops, he must train a portion of his troops to retreat on signal, feigning disorganization. He must also do something about strengthening his remaining troops for if the bluff retreat works the enemy would have greater strength to throw against his troops left in place who will have to hold the enemy off until the envelopment troops have attacked the flank or the rear. The envelopment troops, after running away, will have to be reformed out of sight of the enemy perhaps in a declivity or behind a topographical structure. Then at the right moment the commander would signal for those troops to attack the designated undefended spot in the enemy's formation. The hope would that the enemy would be so disorganized as a result of that attack that it could be defeated. The result is a complicated sequence that would have to be learned, particularly the part about faking rout but being able to regroup on short notice. It also requires judgment on the part of the commander as to when to order the break off the contact between the enveloping troops and when to have them reenter the battle. This is the type of tactic that could be taught in a matter of weeks and possibly in a matter of days.

On the other hand, consider a common weapon used in most of the battles of the first twenty-six or so centuries of the period under discussion, the bow and arrow. The bow and arrow was a weapon that was invented before the dawn of history, perhaps as an outgrowth of the sling but more probably by a person putting a bent piece of wood together with an animal sinew and a sapling for an arrow. In a sense it may simply have replaced the thrown rock as the long-range weapon at some point in the Paleolithic Era. Whatever the birth its first use was probably not warfare but hunting and probably bird hunting. The use initially against birds seems likely because the force that would be available to propel an arrow under these circumstances would be very weak. Since birds are very soft targets and because they would be perched in trees fairly close to the ground and thus close to the archer, they were obvious initial targets. As the technology of bows and arrows improved with better wood for the bows, better material for the bowstrings and the very useful concept of heavy flint points on the arrow to improve the balance of the arrow as well as making it more deadly, the possibility of the bow and arrow becoming a weapon of war became a certainty. The evolution of the bow and arrow into a weapon of war obviously took quite some time.

In addition to the gradual improvement of what might be called the conventional bow at least three other types of bows were invented during the period of the primacy of bow and arrow warfare, all of which would seem to qualify as winners of armament races in their own time and area. The first came out of the plains of central Asia and was used by the mounted soldiers who needed a different kind of bow. They needed a bow that was both small so it could be handled while riding and powerful enough to kill their enemies. With a conventional bow, power was a function of the strength of the bow and the length of the bow. Somewhere in the steppes of central Asia someone invented the compound bow. This was a bow that had multiple curves rather than the simple curve of a conventional bow. The compound bow had, in its central portion, the usual curve but toward the ends of the bow it curved the other direction. While it was harder to draw than a conventional bow of a similar length it produced more power to be applied to the arrow thus giving the rider the ability to shoot at longer ranges than a mounted man with a conventional bow of a similar size. The mounted troops from the steppes had other advantages; good horses, good military training, good horsemanship and good leadership, but their compound bows were of great value to their prowess in war.

Somewhat later than the development of the compound bow in the East, its antithesis was developed in the West. The longbow came out of Britain. The longbow was a conventional bow but of larger size. This was not a new invention but rather an evolution of an idea that was thousands of years old. It was different in that it was a very powerful bow that required strong and accurate bowmen. Years of training were required to master the longbow but if done those archers were a serious long-range force on the battlefield. They were so dangerous to their enemies, often the French, that if captured they sometimes had their first and second fingers on their right hands lopped off, preventing them from plying their dangerous trade.[85] The longbow men were a major factor on the battlefields of Western Europe but only for a relatively short time, eventually being displaced by firearms as that arm became more perfected. That displacement took longer than one might have suspected. The longbow not only had a significant range advantage over personal firearms for centuries but the archer could launch half a dozen or more aimed arrows in the time that it took a soldier with a musket to load, aim and fire his shorter-ranged weapon.

The final derivative of the original bow was the crossbow. The crossbow was made up of a short and very stiff bow with a strong bowstring. The bow was mounted horizontally and perpendicular to a heavy piece of timber. The bow was aimed by sighting down the timber. The bow was so stiff that it could not be bent by pulling back the bowstring. Instead a small winch built into the bow was manually cranked by the archer which drew the bowstring back the requisite distance and locked it in place. The arrow to be fired (in this

---

85 There is some thought that the V-for-victory sign with those two fingers arose when the English archers made the sign to their foes to show them that they were still intact and well able to handle their longbows.

application called a bolt) was inserted and fired by a trigger mechanism. The crossbow had both significant advantages and disadvantages over the other less mechanical bows. The crossbow was very powerful but at the cost of a very short range and a very slow reloading time because of the time it took for the archer to wind the bowstring up to the required tension. It was easily aimed by sighting down the timber base but it was much heavier than, for example, a longbow and its bolts were heavier than the longbow arrows. One of its great advantages was that a soldier could learn to use it without the long training period required for other bows although the training period was still far longer than the training period needed to train troops to execute an envelopment. The ballista, a heavy artillery version of the crossbow, had longer range and fired a much heavier bolt but was not very mobile.

The training period for the commanders ordering envelopments, on the other hand, was rather serious although not necessarily long. Timing was the most important aspect of commanding an envelopment, as was the case for most battlefield maneuvers, and instinct rather than training or experience was likely to be the most useful guide for a commander for he would be looking at a very fluid tactical situation involving a number of variables.

The evolution of weapons was rather a different matter. Weapons did evolve during that thirty-century period but not a great deal and only quite sporadically. In the early part of the period there were changes from the clubs, swords, shields, spears and armor. Bows and arrows of various kinds became more common, new metals (iron and, rarely, steel) became available to the armament industry, new designs of armor and other innovations gradually found their way into armies. The mere fact that a new type of weapon was invented in some part of the world, the compound bow, for example, did not mean that every archer began to use it. First, the word of the invention had to be spread. Second, the potential users of the weapon had to feel that it was an improvement for their purposes over the bow they had been using and were comfortable with. Third, they had to learn how to make and repair the weapon. Fourth, they had to learn how to use the weapon effectively. Finally, they had to make any necessary changes in their battle tactics to use this new weapon to their best advantage. All in all it might take a generation or more to make effective use of the new weapon. On the other hand, changes in tactics were generally much easier and quicker to put into use. Thus warfare went on for thousands of years with some changes in tactics, often governed by the terrain involved, but with few major changes in weapons.

This changed dramatically in the mid-nineteenth century beginning with the building of the French battleship *La Gloire* in 1859 as described earlier. *La Gloire* and her sister ships were iron coated battleships which clearly won a naval armament race and were presumably the most powerful ships in the world although their armor was never tested in battle. A battleship was the most complicated weapon at the time but the French had built them quite rapidly. The British response, HMS *Warrior*, was perhaps somewhat more complicated and was completed the year after *La Gloire*, taking away the French potential advantage in sea power. Two years later CSS *Virginia*, an even more powerful and seemingly invincible ironclad, was put into war service also as described earlier. Her period of supremacy in battle lasted only one day but during that one day she had won a very important armament race and used her advantage to do great damage to several Union ships. By the next day USS *Monitor* had arrived on site and fought *Virginia* to a draw. As is obvious from these two armament races the time necessary for the creation of a new and powerful weapon, even of a very complicated type, had shrunk dramatically as had the of response to such a weapon.[86] This was a trend that continued and accelerated until the 1990s.

---

86 The rapid construction of these ships was not due to their relative simplicity as compared to later and much more complicated vessels. Half a century later the building of the far more complicated and innovative HMS *Dreadnought* in a year was an indication of how fast a powerful nation could react in a time of its own perceived military necessity as was also the rapid production of a weapon that could hardly have been conceived much less constructed few years earlier, the atomic bomb.

Not only had the pace of appearance of new armaments increased in the late nineteenth and twentieth centuries, those new armaments were developed over short periods. Those periods were not generally as short as the development periods of *La Gloire* and *Virginia* nor were the responses as rapid as those of *Warrior* and *Monitor* but it would probably be fair to say that an average time from conception to operational status ranged somewhere between three and six years. Of course the pressure of contemporary wars or of contemplated wars spurred on both the invention and implementation of new and more effective methods of disposing of one's enemies and destroying their military equipment. It was not until 1991 after the collapse of the Soviet Union that at least the United States felt itself free of major threats to its territory and its citizens. It was only from the Soviet Union that any possible armament race could have come. That is not to say, of course, that smaller and weaker countries could not cause trouble for the United States. They could and did. The response to those attacks could only be a combination of intelligence and tactics, a combination that, in spite the application of staggering amounts of money, the United States has yet to perfect. The Osprey was conceived and begun during the last gasp of the Cold War. Instead of discontinuing the program when the Cold War wound down, the Marines took it over from the Army. It did seem to be something that would be more useful to the Marines and their typical operations but, as was clear from the excerpt from the Air Force description of the proposed uses for its Ospreys, the Air Force also saw uses for them. In any case the needs for the Ospreys while felt generally to be necessary for the international situation going forward the needs of the various services were not thought to be particularly pressing. It was well that the needs were not, in fact, very pressing because of a host of problems which cropped up during the development stages. Although those problems were eventually solved as were those of its feathered namesake, all of this contributed to the extraordinary development time and expense. The real significance of the Osprey in the face of great adversity, development time, expense and expenditures of human life was not that it had set records of highly dubious value in those categories. It was rather that, in spite of those enormous negatives, the Osprey had survived them and became operational. Time will tell whether that result was because of justifiable perseverance in the face of great difficulties or because of simple stubbornness on the part of its sponsors. It can only be hoped that the Osprey will turn out to be worth the time, the money and the lives that have been spent to develop it.

To conclude with one last corruption of Mr. Dickens' work, the Marines certainly hope that they will be able to say of their Osprey (fabricated) that it is a far, far better thing that it will do than it has ever done.

Author Biography

Gordon B. Greer was born in Butler, Pennsylvania, and was educated at Phillips Exeter Academy, Harvard College and Harvard Law School. He practiced law for 43 years and also served in the United States Air Force from which he retired as a Major. Mr. Greer lives in Belmont, Massachusetts.